STUART BROAD

ENGLAND CRICKETER

MR VIVEK KUMAR PANDEY SHAMBHUNATH

ISBN 979-888591030-9

Disclaimer : During Writing This Book No character & No religious , No Relation Members Are Harmed. It's Only For Study & Entertainment Purpose. Do Not Take Seriously. Short Biopic Written In This Book Written By Mr Vivek Kumar Pandey.

Contents

Foreword	*vii*
Preface	*ix*
1. Stuart Broad	1
2. England Cricket Team	17
3. History Of The England Cricket	34
4. What Is Cricket ?	48

Foreword

Short biography of Stuart Broad and about life.During writing this book No character & No religious are harmed written by Mr Vivek Kumar Pandey. winner youngest writer award 1st rank in india 2020.He is only one writer can publish 890+ own book that was greatest successfull in his life.This All Credit Goes To My Super Hero Daddy.

Preface

Author biography in English :MY NAME IS VIVEK KUMAR PANDEY . I WAS BORN IN 30 SEP 2002,I AM FROM SURAT GUJARAT INDIA.MY DREAM WAS TO BE GOOD WRITERS ,MY FAMILY SUPPORTED ME TO SUCCESSFUL AND I CAN DO IT MY SELF.How do I write? That is a question, I believe, that can be honestly answered by me."CELEBRATING YOUNGEST WRITER AWARD WINNER IN GUJARAT 1ST RANK" MR PANDEY JI . I may think I did a good job writing something . The reader is the one who decides the quality of my writing. I do find writing to be natural to me and therefore find it to be a real challenge. My trick as a challenged writer is to do the best I can and know that I am happy with the final outcome. It may take a while to do my best and there may be quite a few problems I run into along the way.

I am not a greedy person those who are thinking about me and my self I never tried it anyone people suffering from sadness ,I trying to get promoted people suffering from happiness and joy in your Life Time. Now in current situation in India and also world people are unemployed and have no many but our indian governor help to people to get free food from ration card , i also take part in leadership team ,i am Motivational speaker , Film script writer. There was my two dream firstly writer and secondly actor & also my own film is upcoming soon i done almost completely completed script for my film .I AM GOING TO SAY WORD OF HEART TOUCH OUT PLEASE READ IT" , firstly i thanks my father he supports me in this field they always getting inspired me by own his words and behavior ,they always said that he was a biggest person in the world in future and also they purchase fruit and chocolate for me in anytime & anyway , firstly my father buy him then call me Vivek you want a chocolate i will say yes papa but how many tell me ,papa: you tell me how much i buy him i told 1 or 2 chocolate but my father purchase whole the boxes of chocolate and they get suprised me. MY FATHER WAS BORN IN " 20 SEPTEMBER" 1971 IN INDIA.

1) MY FATHER FAVORITE CLOTHES IS KURTA PAIJMA AND ALSO STYLES SHOE

2) FAVORITE SINGER IS KISHORE DA

3) FAVORITE STATE GUJARAT AND KOLKATA , HIS VILLAGE IN BIHAR

4) FAVORITE COLOR BLACK AND WHITE

THEY ALSO LOVE cricket like IPL and one day t-20 .they also like watching a News daily and heard the song daily ,they also interested in tik tok video but in current time tik tok is banned in india but also few videos are in you tube. In lockdown time my family and me very enjoy day daily. my father play daily ludo with his sister and son, daughter.they always loved tea and coffee anytime call me "I . I make it tea for my father but some reason after the April to june they are suffering from fever and cough , weakness on 6 June 2020 my father death. they not told me say bye bye his life. After death of 6 June on 10 june my mom and dad anniversary.but my father is Best in the world they can do anything for me please take care of father and respect it of your parents.

CHAPTER ONE

Stuart Broad

- *Stuart Broad*

1. Disclaimer : Disclaimer : During Writing This Book No character & No religious , No Relation Members Are Harmed. It's Only For Study & Entertainment Purpose. Do Not Take Seriously,Written By Mr Vivek Kumar Pandey.

Stuart Christopher John Broad (born 24 June 1986) is an English cricketer who plays Test cricket for the England cricket team and a former One Day and Twenty 20 International captain. He is widely considered to be one of the best fast bowlers of his generation.

A right-arm seam bowler and left-handed batsman, Broad began his professional career at Leicestershire; in 2008 he transferred to Nottinghamshire, the county of his birth and the team for which his father played. In August 2006 he was voted the Cricket Writers' Club Young Cricketer of the Year. In the fourth Test of the 2015 Ashes series Broad took career best figures of 8–15 in the Australian first innings as they were dismissed for just 60. This performance was named as Wisden's Men's Test spell of the decade.

Broad was awarded the Man of the Match in the fifth Test of the 2009 Ashes series at the Oval, after figures of 5/37 in the afternoon session of the second day. On 30 July 2011, at the Nottingham Test match against India, he achieved a Test match hat-trick in the process gaining his then best Test figures of 6–46. As a batsman, he holds the second-highest ever Test score made by a number 9, scoring 169 against Pakistan in August 2010. At the start of the summer in 2012 Broad, returning from injury, produced figures of 7 for 72 in a match haul of 11 wickets against the West Indies. He is

England's second highest wicket taker in Test cricket.

On the morning of the fifth and final day of the third Test of the 2020 series against the West Indies, Broad became the seventh bowler to take 500 wickets in Test cricket, after dismissing Kraigg Brathwaite. Broad was the fourth fast bowler, and second bowler for England to reach the milestone after James Anderson, who achieved it against the same batsman. In December 2021, in the second match of the 2021–22 Ashes series, Broad played in his 150th Test match.

- *Stuart Broad life*

Broad was born 12 weeks prematurely and his life was saved by a doctor called John, after whom he was (middle) named when he survived. Broad originally started his cricketing career as an opening batsman, following in the footsteps of his father, the former England opener and current ICC match referee Chris Broad. It was not until he was 17 and had a growth spurt that he started to consider being a fast bowler. Broad had been associated with Leicestershire since he was 8 years old, having represented them at Under-9 level, and played for Melton Mowbray club Egerton Park, which also produced England seamer Tim Munton. Broad played for Egerton Park from the ages of 9 to 19; in his final two seasons he opened the batting with fellow Leicestershire player Matthew Boyce and spearheaded the attack. He was awarded the Leicestershire Young Cricketers Batsman Award in 1996.

At the age of 16, he considered himself better at field hockey and played as a goalkeeper, for Leicestershire and the Midlands, and had a trial with an England underage team. At the age of 17, he had a growth spurt and converted from a batsman to a seam bowler.

- *Stuart Broad Education*

Broad was educated at Brooke Priory School and Oakham School, a co-educational independent school in the market town of Oakham in Rutland, where he was in the same year as England Rugby back-row Tom Croft. Broad finished his school career with three B grades at A-level, and was given the choice of a place at Durham University or a contract with Leicestershire County Cricket Club.

- *Stuart Broad Domestic career*

Broad played his first game for Leicestershire 2nd XI in 2004 just before his 18th birthday and impressed enough to be given a full contract for the following season. Broad continued to impress Director of Cricket James Whitaker and made his first-class debut early in the 2005 season against Durham University Centre of Cricketing Excellence. He returned credible figures of 1/40 from 15 overs. His maiden first-class wicket was that of Nick Lamb. Broad followed this appearance with his first County Championship appearance against Somerset at the familiar location of Oakham.

In the 2006 season Broad took his first 5 wicket haul against championship favourites Surrey and scored his first championship 50 against Derbyshire. His most eye-catching performances were in the Twenty20 Cup, where his economy of 4.50 was the second-best of the season of bowlers with more than 15 overs bowled. In the County Championship Broad played twelve of Leicestershire's 13 matches until called up for England, and his 44 wickets at an average of 31.38 meant he led his county both in terms of wickets and bowling average. On 23 August 2007 it was announced that Broad would be leaving Leicestershire at the end of the season to join Nottinghamshire, after choosing not to renew his contract and to return to his home county. In the 2013 season, Broad played in the final of the Yorkshire Bank 40 tournament. He was out for a duck and got three wickets in his last over wrapping up the game against Glamorgan. Broad was apart of the Nottinghamshire side that beat Surrey in the final of the Royal London One Day Cup in 2017 played at Lords.

- *Stuart Broad International career*

Broad played for the England Under-19 squad in 2005, facing the Sri Lankan Under-19 squad, and took five for seventeen in the first 'Test' at Shenley.He was named in the ECB National Academy squad for the winter of 2005–06 and was then called up to the England 'A' squad touring the West Indies, as a replacement for James Anderson, who had been drafted into the Test side touring India. In April 2006, Broad was again called up to the England A squad, facing the touring Sri Lankan team.

Broad was also included in the ECB's 25-man development squad for the 2006 season. David Graveney, the chairman of selectors, said, "The squad essentially enables the England Head Coach (Duncan Fletcher), working with his support staff and the National Academy staff, to monitor more closely the development of international players and better prepare them for the demands of the international game."

- *Broad playing against Pakistan in the 3rd ODI at the Rose Bowl in 2006*

On 23 August 2006, Broad was included in the England one-day squad for the one-day internationals against Pakistan, and a couple of days later was named Young Cricketer of the Year by the Cricket Writers' Club.On 28 August, Broad made his first England appearance, in the Twenty20 International against Pakistan. Broad bowled four overs for 35 runs, and took two wickets in two balls, Shoaib Malik and Younis Khan, and narrowly missed out on a hat-trick, after a lofted shot from Shahid Afridi fell just short of Kevin Pietersen. On 30 August, he made his ODI debut, taking a wicket in his first over, as well as being involved in a last-wicket partnership of 29 with Darren Gough. In the third ODI on 5 September 2006, Broad once again found himself on a hat-trick with the wickets of Abdul Razzaq and Kamran Akmal, but again missed out on the third. He bowled ten overs and ended with figures of three for 57 with one maiden.

- *Stuart Broad in 2007: West Indies, India, T20 World Cup and Sri Lanka*

Broad was left out of the squad for the 2006 ICC Champions Trophy and the 2006-07 Commonwealth Bank Series. However, he was called up for the finals in the latter following injuries to Jon Lewis and Chris Tremlett. He was also called into England's squad as a replacement partway through the 2007 World Cup. He finished the tournament by scoring the winning runs in England's final match against the West Indies.

Broad also featured in the ODI squad at the end of the West Indies tour of England in summer 2007, taking three for twenty in the first match to take England to a 1–0 lead in the ODI series. In the second ODI he took 2–49 but England lost the match by 61 runs. Broad was expensive in the final match of the series, conceding 71 runs for no wickets.

He took his first wicket against India in the ODI against them in the second match at Bristol. On 30 August, he took career-best bowling figures of four for 51 as England bowled out India for 212 in the fourth match of the summer's ODI series. Broad also hit an unbeaten 45 to take his first ODI Man of the Match award. The definitive unbeaten partnership of 99 runs he shared with Ravi Bopara is a record eighth-wicket stand for England in ODIs. He bowled poorly in the next match, taking 1–84 as India won by 38 runs. He took 2–46 at the Oval but India narrowly won the match by 2 runs.

Broad took 1–29 in the opening match of the 2007 world T20 against Zimbabwe. He followed this up by taking 0–23 against Australia as England lost by eight wickets. He took 3–37 against South Africa but England suffered another defeat, this time by 19 runs. He took 1–35 against New Zealand but could not prevent another defeat for England.

On 19 September 2007, Indian batsman Yuvraj Singh hit six sixes from one Broad over in a group match at Kingsmead Cricket Ground in Durban, South Africa, during 2007's ICC World Twenty20. The 36-runs from the Broad over helped Yuvraj Singh make the quickest 50 in international cricket, off just 12 balls. Referring to this rare occurrence as "Yuvraj's magic moment", Phil Long of BBC's Test Match Special blogged: "Every so often you have to take off your England sunhat, sit back and enjoy a once-in-lifetime 'I was there' moment." This was the fourth time the feat had been performed in senior cricket and the first time in Twenty20 cricket. The performance was not repeated in any form of international cricket against a Test-playing nation until Kieron Pollard did the same against Sri Lanka in a T20 International in 2021.

Broad enjoyed a hugely successful ODI series in Sri Lanka in October 2007, taking eleven wickets in the series at an average of 19.27. He took figures of 2–54 in the first match and followed this up with 2–42 in the second match. In the third match of the series Broad made an unbeaten 20 with the bat and took another two wickets. In the final match of the series he took 3–36 and although England lost the match by over 100 runs, they won the series three-two to record its first ever ODI series win in Sri Lanka. This resulted in Broad making his Test debut against Sri Lanka; in a high scoring game, he took a single wicket, conceding 95 runs in the process as the match ended in a draw.

- *Stuart Broad 2008: New Zealand, South Africa and India*

Broad went on to have an equally successful ODI series against New Zealand. Although England fell to a three-one defeat, Broad was the leading wicket taker and held the highest batting average, 52, in the England team. During the tour of New Zealand in 2008, Broad, along with Alastair Cook and James Anderson, posed naked for the Cosmopolitan paper with just a cricket bat for cover. England won the first Test against New Zealand by 121 runs, with Broad taking figures of 3–54 to help England win the game.

In the first Test against New Zealand on home soil, Broad took three wickets in the match. England won the second match by six wickets, although Broad picked up no wickets in the match. On 6 June 2008, Broad scored his maiden Test fifty, against New Zealand at Trent Bridge, making 64 before being bowled by Chris Martin. In the first ODI against New Zealand Broad took 2–14, before taking another two wickets in the final match of the series, conceding fifty runs in the process.

He made his second Test fifty in July 2008, in the Test series against South Africa, scoring a new best of 76. In the Second Test at Headingley, Broad contributed seventeen runs in the first innings, as England was bowled out on the first day for 203. In the second innings, with the match already lost, Broad top-scored with 67 in an innings that included some impressive drives through midwicket and cover, giving further evidence of his batsmanship.

After this, his Test batting average briefly rose above 40. His performances with the bat at the time led pundits to suggest that he may become a genuine all rounder, with Geoffrey Boycott comparing him to Garfield Sobers: "He's a wonderful player. There's a little bit of Sobers in him". Broad was surprisingly dropped for the following Test at Edgbaston, making way for the returning Paul Collingwood. England captain Michael Vaughan said he was left out because of his bowling, but the decision has been criticised: Collingwood was no better a bowler than Broad, and Broad's batsmanship quite encouraging. Broad duly took seven wickets for Nottinghamshire against Durham while the Test was being played.

On 26 August 2008, he recorded the first five-wicket haul in his international career with best figures of five for 23 against South Africa at his home ground in the second ODI of the series, with England winning the series 4–0 with Broad taking 8 wickets within the series at an average of 18.4 and shooting up to 4th in the ICC ODI world rankings, the highest in his career and the best by any English bowler since Andrew Flintoff in 2003.

In the second ODI against India Broad performed well, taking figures of 4–55. He took 1–36 in the next match as England lost by 18 runs. In the final match of the series he took 1–54, but England lost again, this time by six wickets. In the second Test against India, Broad was ineffectual with the ball. He took 1–84 in an India's first innings before taking 1–50 in India's second innings as the match ended in a draw.

- *Stuart Broad in 2009: West Indies and T20 World Cup*

On 26 May 2009, Broad was named Man of the Series (one-day) against the West Indies in England. He took a total of six wickets, and England won the series two-nil after the first ODI was rained out. In the adjacent Test series, in which the home side fairly routed its opponents, Broad's wickets came at an average of just eighteen – "further evidence," reckoned journalist Nick Hoult, "of the top class international cricketer that lurks within. His bowling, particularly the variety he has added to his game, makes him a potential Ashes star ."

On 5 June 2009, Netherlands defeated England by four wickets in the first match of the ICC World Twenty20. The Netherlands needed seven to win from the final over with Broad bowling. He spurned two run-out opportunities from the first two balls, and dropped a catch off the third. The Dutch needed two runs from the final ball to win, and got them after Broad picked up the ball in his follow through and, attempting to win the match, overthrew, missing his third run-out opportunity of the over and allowing the batsmen to come back for the match-clinching second run. in the next match against Pakistan, he took 3–17 to help England win by 48 runs. England also beat India by 3 runs. Although Broad failed to take a wicket, he bowled his four overs for just 21 runs to help England secure a narrow victory. England lost their final game of the tournament against the West Indies, with Broad taking 1–20.

- *Broad celebrates the wicket of Michael Hussey with Graeme Swann in the 3rd Test of the 2009 Ashes Series.*

In July 2009, Broad was named in The Ashes squad to face Australia for the first Test at the SWALEC Stadium, Cardiff – his maiden Ashes Test. He scored a 22-ball 19 in England's first-innings total of 435, but in 32 overs he took just one wicket (that of Michael Clarke, caught behind for 83) as Australia amassed 674 for 6 declared, with four centurions. Nonetheless, his final-day 14 proved crucial, keeping the Australians at bay alongside Paul Collingwood for a minute over an hour before James Anderson and Monty Panesar blocked out the final 11½ overs to salvage an unlikely draw.

The second Test at Lord's saw Broad take three wickets, including the important wicket of Australian skipper Ricky Ponting, bowled off an inside-edged cut for 38 as England pursued victory, and took a diving outfield catch to remove the opener Simon Katich in the first innings, as England took a 1–0 lead in the series.

Though he took no wickets in the first innings of the third Test at Edgbaston, Broad hit a 64-ball 55 to extend England's first-innings lead to 114. On the final day, Broad took two of the three wickets to fall: Mike Hussey for 64 and, late in the day, Marcus North for 96. Nonetheless, Australia drew the match with ease.

In the fourth Test at Headingley, Broad took his place in an England first-innings collapse, clipping Stuart Clark to square leg for 3 as Australia's seam attack bowled England out for 102. As Australia scored 445, Broad took six wickets for 91 in Australia's only innings, at that time his best first-class innings return, and in the second innings contributed a rapid 61 from 48 balls, though he could not avert an innings defeat.

England therefore started the fifth Test at the Oval with the series level at 1–1, with a victory required to secure the Ashes. He took 5 for 37 in the afternoon session of the second day, taking five of the first seven wickets to fall to take the Australian innings from 73/0 to 111/7 and eventually 160 all out. He also contributed 37 and 29 with the bat, and on the final day took the wicket of Shane Watson lbw for 40, the second wicket to fall in consecutive overs to start Australia's collapse, winning the Man of the Match award as England won by 197 runs to regain the Ashes 2–1.

He finished the tour with an aggregate of 234 runs and 18 wickets, leading England's bowling figures both in wickets taken and in bowling average (30.22). Though three Australian bowlers took more wickets, Broad was the only bowler from either side to claim two five-wicket innings hauls during the series.

- *Stuart Broad in 2009: ICC Champions Trophy*

This was a good tournament for Broad. He was the second highest wicket taker overall throughout the tournament with 10 wickets in 3 matches, only behind Wayne Parnell who took 11 in the same number of matches. In the first match of the tournament against Sri Lanka he took 3–49 in a winning effort. He followed it up with a 3–67 vs South Africa, putting England through to the semi finals. He then took 4–39 vs New Zealand in a losing effort after England had already been bowled out for 146, with New Zealand making the runs in just 27.1 overs. This was his last game in the tournament with Broad picking up an injury that kept him out of the semi finals, which

England lost to Australia.

- *Stuart Broad in 2009–10: South Africa*

Broad's injuries continued through to the tour of South Africa, keeping him out of the two twenty20 matches, which both ended up being abandoned. The weather affected the 1st One Day International which was probably an advantage for Broad and the England team with Broad being fit for the 3rd ODI, with England winning the second ODI by 7 wickets after Paul Collingwood and Jonathan Trott had a partnership of 162 with Collingwood getting 105.

When Broad returned he instantly made an impact with numerous wickets but turned out to be very expensive. With his first game getting figures of 4–71, England suffered defeat by 112 runs. Broad improved on his economy rate in the 4th ODI with figures of 2–30 from 9.5 overs. This backed up James Anderson who took 5–23. The final game was rained off before a ball was bowled to leave England with a 2–1 victory and only the second team to win a one-day series vs South Africa in South Africa.

Broad struggled in the First test in Centurion with only taking 1–74 in the first innings and 2–54 in the second. His batting was unsuccessful, getting only 17 and a duck. The duck was during a dramatic collapse where England went from 205–4 to 218–9 with Graham Onions batting out the final over to save the test.

In the second test Broad showed good form with the ball with 2–44 in the first innings but then taking 4–43 in the second dismissing Jacques Kallis, AB de Villiers and JP Duminy all within 3 overs. He took the wicket of Mark Boucher the next day to leave Graeme Swann to dismiss the rest of the South African line up. This gave England an innings and 98 run victory. After this test Broad went up to 7th in the ICC Test bowling rankings, the highest in his career. During this tour he declined to play in the IPL with James Anderson on the grounds he wanted to focus on his Test cricket first, and feared injury in the IPL.

- *Broad bowling against Sri Lanka at Lord's in June 2011*

Broad had an indifferent tour of Australia, which was cut short due to injury. He started with a half-century in a warm-up game, and overall took 6 wickets over the two games against Western Australia and South Australia.

In the first Test at the Gabba, Brisbane, he fell for a golden duck in England's innings, the final victim of Peter Siddle's hat-trick. Wicketless in Australia's first innings, he had Simon Katich caught in the second as the Test was drawn. In the second Test at Adelaide, he finished Australia's first innings off with the wicket of Brad Haddin, but a stomach muscle injury limited his participation in the second where England won by an innings. That injury was revealed to be a muscle tear, and it ruled Broad out of the remaining three Tests and the one-day series that followed. He was not missed for the rest of the Test series but he was for the ODIs because England were plagued by injuries throughout the 6–1 series defeat.

- *Stuart Broad in 2013: New Zealand and Ashes series*

Broad comes in to bowl during the England v Australia game of the 2013 ICC Champions Trophy at Edgbaston.On the fifth day of the 3rd Test against New Zealand, Broad set a new record for the longest time spent at the crease without scoring a run, with 103 minutes out in the middle, facing 62 balls. The previous record was 101 minutes set by New Zealander Geoff Allott against South Africa in 1999.

On 19 May, in the First Test against New Zealand at Lord's, Broad took career best figures of 7/44 in the second innings of the match. In England's second innings, he also contributed 26 runs to their total of 213.

In the first Test of the 2013 Ashes held at Trent Bridge, Broad stood his ground after being given not out when edging an Ashton Agar delivery which deflected off wicket-keeper Brad Haddin's gloves and was caught by Australia captain Michael Clarke at first slip; the Umpire Decision Review System was in use during the series, but Australia had used all of its challenges when the incident occurred. Although neither the rules nor common practice required Broad to walk, he drew heavy criticism from many observers who thought his edge was too thick to have reasonably stood his ground.

Broad was on 37 at the time of the incident and went to make 65, sharing a partnership of 138 with Ian Bell. England went on to win the match by 14 runs with Broad taking the wickets of Shane Watson and Clarke in Australia's second innings. Australia coach Darren Lehmann was later fined 20% of his match fee for calling Broad a cheat on Australian radio, and in doing so inciting Australian crowds to boo Broad in future English tours of Australia.

On 2 August 2013, Broad took his 200th Test wicket, bowling Clarke in the first innings of the drawn third Ashes Test at Old Trafford.

In the fourth Test, at the Riverside Ground in Chester-le-Street, Broad took eleven wickets with two five-wicket hauls and was named man of the match as England ensured a series win. In the first innings, he took 5–71, including a spell of 3–12 in the morning session of day 2 where he removed David Warner, Usman Khawaja and Clarke to reduce Australia to 49–3. In their second innings, chasing 299 to win, Australia had made 174–3 when Broad took the wicket Clarke for the fifth time in the series, with the first delivery after a drinks break. In this spell he took 6–20 from 45 balls, including the final Australian wicket, to bowl Australia out for 224 and win the match by 74 runs. Broad ended the match with his best test bowling match figures of 11–121.

- *Stuart Broad in 2013–14: Ashes series*

Broad was England's leading wicket taker in the first Test of the 2013–14 Ashes series at the Gabba in Brisbane, taking 6–81 in the first innings and ending with match figures of 8–136, in the match that England lost in four days by 381 runs. In the second Test Broad took 3–98 in Australia's first innings, but as England struggled he only bowled six overs in the second innings as Australia romped to victory. Broad took 3–100 in the third Test but was then injured by a delivery from Mitchell Johnson, which dismissed him for just 5.

The injury prevented him from bowling in the second innings, as England went on to lose the game and the series. Broad was declared fit for the fourth Test and took 3–45 in the Australian first innings, but struggled in the second, bowling 10 wicketless overs for 58 runs. In the final Test, Broad batted well, making an unbeaten 30 in the first innings and then 42 in the second. England went on to lose the game and the series 5–0, leading to the England team being heavily criticised. Despite this, Broad was one of the few members of the team to come out of the series with any credibility.

- *Stuart Broad in 2014: West Indies, T20 World Cup, Sri Lanka and India*

Broad continued as captain for the tour of the West Indies. This included three ODIs and three T20Is. In the ODI series England won 2–1, with Broad bringing England home in the 2nd game with a knock of 28 not out. In the third game he took 2–58 as England won by 25 runs. He only played in the first T20I, as England lost by 27 runs, taking figures of 0–26.

Broad was named captain of the England cricket team for the 2014 ICC World Twenty20 in Bangladesh. He did not take a wicket in the first two games, as England lost to New Zealand and beat Sri Lanka. In the third game, against South Africa, Broad took 1–33 but England lost the match to end their hopes of qualifying for the next stage. He took 3–24 against the Netherlands, but he was unable to prevent an embarrassing defeat for England.

- *Stuart Broad in 2015: Tri-Series, World Cup, West Indies and New Zealand*

Following an injury which had kept him out of the one-day tour of Sri Lanka, Broad returned for the Tri-Series against Australia and India. In the first match of the series he was wicket less as England lost to Australia. In the next match against India, Broad finished with figures of 0–33. His worst performance of the series came in the following match against Australia, where he finished with figures of 0–61. However, he played well in the must win game against India, taking figures of 2–56 to help England qualify for the final.In the final match against Australia he took figures of 3–55 and made 24 with the bat, but it was not enough to prevent an England defeat as they went on to finish the tournament as runners-up.

Broad took figures of 2–66 in England's opening game loss to Australia. In the following game against New Zealand, he was unimpressive as England suffered a humiliating eight wicket defeat. He failed to take a wicket against Scotland as England won their first match of the tournament, and also finished wicket less as England suffered a nine wicket defeat against Sri Lanka, meaning he had failed to take a wicket in his past three matches. He finished with 1–52 in England's must win game against Bangladesh, but was dismissed for 9 as England lost the game to bow out of the tournament at the group stage. He finished with figures of 1–18 against Afghanistan in a rain affected as England won their final match of the tournament by nine wickets.

The first match against the West Indies, Broad took 2–67 in their first innings to help restrict them to 295. However, in the second innings he could only manage to take one wicket as the West Indies held on for a draw. In the second Test ok 4–61 in West Indies first innings to help out England in a strong position. He took another wicket in the second innings as England forced a result to go 1–0 up in the series. In the first Test Broad took 1–31 in West Indies first innings to help England into a lead. However, England collapsed in their second innings and Broad himself was out for a duck. He took 1–29 in the West Indies second innings but it wasn't enough to prevent a five wicket defeat as the West Indies levelled the series at 1–1.

In the two match series against New Zealand, Broad took 3–77 in New Zealand's first innings. With New Zealand chasing a big score to win the match, Broad took 3–50 in New Zealand's second innings to help England win by 124 runs and go 1–0 up in the series. Broad took 5–109 in New Zealand's first innings of the next Test, although he went at an economy rate of over six an over. He made 46 with the bat to help England level the scores after the first innings. He took 2–94 in the second innings but was again expensive, and New Zealand went on to win the match and tie the series 1–1.

- *Stuart Broad in 2015: Ashes series*

In Australia's first innings of the first Test, Broad took figures of 2–60 and followed this up by taking 3–39 in their second innings as England won the match to take the lead in the series. Broad took 4–83 in Australia's first innings of the second Test but they built a large first innings score of 566. Broad did not take a wicket in the Australians second innings as they won by 405 runs. In the third Test Broad took 2–44 in Australia's first innings and also took a wicket in their second as England won the game to regain the lead. In the fourth Test Broad took career best figures of 8–15 in the Australian first innings as they were dismissed for just 60. England went on to win the match convincingly and regain the Ashes. In the final Test Broad did not take a wicket as Australia won by an innings and 48 runs, although England won the series 3–2.

- *Stuart Broad in 2015: Pakistan*

Broad played in the first Test against Pakistan, which was played in the UAE. While Broad only took one wicket in the match, he bowled economically, including bowling eight overs for just eight runs in the second innings. England came to close to forcing a result, but the match ended in a draw. In the second Test Broad again only managed to take one wicket as Pakistan enjoyed a convincing win to go 1–0 up in the three-match series. In the third Test, Broad continued to bowl economically, taking figures of 2–13 from 13 overs in Pakistan's first innings, as they were dismissed for 234. In the second innings, he took 3–44 but England struggled in their second innings and Pakistan went on to win the game to win the series 2–0.

- *Stuart Broad 2015–16: South Africa*

In the first test in South Africa, Broad took figures of 4–25 and 1–29 and hit an unbeaten 32 from just 33 balls as England won by 241 runs. The second game ended in a high scoring draw, with Broad taking 2–94 in South Africa's first innings. In the third Test, Broad took 2–82 in South Africa's first innings in a game which looked to be finely poised. However, in South Africa's second innings, he ripped through their top order, finishing with figures of 6–17. Included in his six wickets were the prized wickets of AB de Villiers and Hashim Amla. England went on to win the game by seven wickets, with the result giving them an unassailable 2–0 series lead. England performed poorly in the final game, with Broad taking three wickets in the match as South Africa secured a victory by a margin of 280 runs, meaning the series finished 2–1 to England. As a result of his performances, Broad became the number one ranked Test bowler in the world.

After not playing for England in limited overs cricket since their poor showing at the 2015 World Cup, Broad was included in the squad for the ODI series against South Africa. He played in the fourth ODI, although he returned expensive figures, finishing up with 1–55 in seven overs, as England lost the game. He was selected in the side for the final game, which proved to be the decider, and although he bowled economically, he did not pick up a wicket and England went on to lose the game and the series 3–2.

- *Stuart Broad in 2016: Sri Lanka, Pakistan, Bangladesh and India*

Broad took figures of 4–21 in Sri Lanka's first innings of the first Test as they were dismissed for just 91. In the second innings he took 1–57 as England won by an innings and 88 runs. In the second match, Broad took 4–40 in Sri Lanka's first innings, but was less effective in their second, finishing with just one wicket, as England won the match by nine wickets. In the final rain affected match of the series, Broad took 2–79 as Sri Lanka were dismissed for 288, but the match ended in a draw due to the bad weather.

Broad took figures of 3–71 in Pakistan's first innings of the first Test, and took 3–38 in their second innings, although Pakistan did enough to secure a 75 run victory. In the second Test Broad took 1–20 in Pakistan's first innings as they were dismissed for 198 and England secured a 330 run victory. In the third Test, Broad took 3–83 in Pakistan's first innings as they reached 400, and then took 2–24 in their second innings to help England secure an unlikely victory after dismissing them for 201. In the final match of the series, Broad was less effective, taking just one wicket in the match, as England lost by 10 wickets.

In the first innings of the first Test against Bangladesh, Broad did not take a wicket in the first innings, although he bowled economically. In the second innings he took figures of 2–31 to help England win by 21 runs. He was rested for the second Test, which England lost

Broad played in the first Test against India, taking figures of 1–78 in the first innings, before taking 0–8 in the second innings as the match ended in a draw. In the second Test he took 1–49 as India made 455 in their first innings. He took 4–33 in the second innings to restrict India to 204 runs, although India won the match by 246 runs. Broad missed the next two Tests through injury, but returned in the fifth Test. He took figures of 2–80 as India scored 759/7 and went on to win the match by an inning and 75 runs to win the series 4–0.

- *Achievements and honours*

1. On 17 September 2015, NET tram 237 was named in honour of Broad.
2. He was appointed a Member of the Order of the British Empire in the 2016 Birthday Honours for services to cricket.
3. At the conclusion of the 5th Test in India's tour of the United Kingdom in 2018, Broad and Anderson had tallied 850 wickets playing together across 111 Tests, third all-time on the list of bowling pairs in Tests, behind only Glenn McGrath and Shane Warne (1,001 wickets in 104 Tests together) and Chaminda Vaas and Muttiah Muralitharan (895 wickets in 95 Tests together).
4. They have subsequently gone on to pass Vaas and Muralitharan, and as of July 2021 they have a combined 928 wickets in 123 Tests played together.

5. On the morning of the fifth and final day of the third Test of the 2020 series against the West Indies, Broad became the seventh bowler to take 500 wickets in Test cricket, after dismissing Kraigg Brathwaite. Broad was the fourth fast bowler, and second bowler for England to reach the milesteone after James Anderson, who achieved it against the same batsman.

CHAPTER TWO

England Cricket Team

- England Cricket Team

1. Disclaimer : During Writing This Book No character & No religious , No Relation Members Are Harmed. It's Only For Study & Entertainment Purpose. Do Not Take Seriously. Short Biopic Written In This Book Written By Mr Vivek Kumar Pandey.

The England cricket team represents England and Wales in international cricket. Since 1997, it has been governed by the England and Wales Cricket Board (ECB), having been previously governed by Marylebone Cricket Club (the MCC) since 1903. England, as a founding nation, is a Full Member of the International Cricket Council (ICC) with Test, One Day International (ODI) and Twenty20 International (T20I) status. Until the 1990s, Scottish and Irish players also played for England as those countries were not yet ICC members in their own right.

England and Australia were the first teams to play a Test match (15–19 March 1877), and along with South Africa, these nations formed the Imperial Cricket Conference (the predecessor to today's International Cricket Council) on 15 June 1909. England and Australia also played the first ODI on 5 January 1971. England's first T20I was played on 13 June 2005, once more against Australia.

As of December 2021, England have played 1,044 Test matches, winning 378 and losing 314 (with 352 draws). In Test series against Australia, England play for The Ashes, one of the most famous trophies in all of sport, and they have won the urn on 32 occasions. England have also played 760 ODIs, winning 383. They have appeared in the final of the Cricket World Cup four times, winning once in 2019; they have also finished as runners-up in two ICC Champions Trophies (2004 and 2013). England have played 143 T20Is, winning 75.They won the ICC T20 World Cup in 2010, and were runners-up in 2016.As of 12 November 2021, England are ranked fourth in Tests, second in ODIs and first in T20Is by the ICC.

- The All-England Eleven in 1846

The first recorded incidence of a team with a claim to represent England comes from 9 July 1739 when an "All-England" team, which consisted of 11 gentlemen from any part of England exclusive of Kent, played against "the Unconquerable County" of Kent and lost by a margin of "very few notches". Such matches were repeated on numerous occasions for the best part of a century.

In 1846 William Clarke formed the All-England Eleven. This team eventually competed against a United All-England Eleven with annual matches occurring between 1847 and 1856. These matches were arguably the most important contest of the English season if judged by the quality of the players.

- Early tours

The first overseas tour occurred in September 1859 with England touring North America. This team had six players from the All-England Eleven, six from the United All-England Eleven and was captained by George Parr.

With the outbreak of the American Civil War, attention turned elsewhere. English tourists visited Australia in 1861–62 with this first tour organised as a commercial venture by Messrs Spiers and Pond, restaurateurs of Melbourne. Most matches played during tours prior to 1877 were "against odds", with the opposing team fielding more than 11 players to make for a more even contest. This first Australian tour were mostly against odds of at least 18/11.

- The first England team to tour southern Australia in 1861–62

The tour was so successful that Parr led a second tour in 1863–64. James Lillywhite led a subsequent England team which sailed on the P&O steamship Poonah on 21 September 1876. They played a combined

Australian XI, for once on even terms of 11-a-side. The match, starting on 15 March 1877 at the Melbourne Cricket Ground came to be regarded as the inaugural Test match. The combined Australian XI won this Test match by 45 runs with Charles Bannerman of Australia scoring the first Test century. At the time, the match was promoted as James Lillywhite's XI v Combined Victoria and New South Wales. The teams played a return match on the same ground at Easter, 1877, when Lillywhite's team avenged their loss with a victory by four wickets. The first Test match on English soil occurred in 1880 with England victorious; this was the first time England fielded a fully representative side with W. G. Grace included in the team.

- 1880s

As a result of this loss, the tour of 1882–83 was dubbed by England captain Ivo Bligh as "the quest to regain the ashes". England, with a mixture of amateurs and professionals, won the series 2–1. Bligh was presented with an urn that contained some ashes, which have variously been said to be of a bail, ball or even a woman's veil, and so The Ashes was born. A fourth match was then played which Australia won by four wickets. However, the match was not considered part of the Ashes series. England dominated many of these early contests with England winning the Ashes series 10 times between 1884 and 1898. During this period England also played their first Test match against South Africa in 1889 at Port Elizabeth.

- 1890s

England won the 1890 Ashes series 2–0, with the third match of the series being the first Test match to be abandoned. England lost 2–1 in the 1891–92 series, although England regained the urn the following year. England again won the 1894–95 series, winning 3–2 under the leadership of Andrew Stoddart. In 1895–96, England played South Africa, winning all Tests in the series. The 1899 Ashes series was the first tour where the MCC and the counties appointed a selection committee. There were three active players: Grace, Lord Hawke and Warwickshire captain Herbert Bainbridge. Prior to this, England teams for home Tests had been chosen by the club on whose ground the match was to be played. England lost the 1899 Ashes series 1–0, with Grace making his final Test appearance in the first match of the series.

- 1900s

The start of the 20th century saw mixed results for England as they lost four of the eight Ashes series between 1900 and 1914. During this period, England lost their first series against South Africa in the 1905–06 season 4–1 as their batting faltered.

England lost their first series of the new century to Australia in 1901–02 Ashes. Australia also won the 1902 series, which was memorable for exciting cricket, including Gilbert Jessop scoring a Test century in just 70 minutes. England regained the Ashes in 1904 under the captaincy of Pelham Warner. R. E. Foster scored 287 on his debut and Wilfred Rhodes took 15 wickets in a match. In 1905–06, England lost 4–1 against South Africa. England avenged the defeat in 1907, when they won the series 1–0 under the captaincy of Foster. However, they lost the 1909 Ashes series against Australia, suing 25 players in the process. England also lost to South Africa, with Jack Hobbs scoring his first of 15 centuries on the tour.

- 1910s

England toured Australia in 1911–12 and beat their opponents 4–1. The team included the likes of Rhodes, Hobbs, Frank Woolley and Sydney Barnes. England lost the first match of the series but bounced back and won the next four Tests. This proved to be the last Ashes series before the war.

The 1912 season saw England take part in a unique experiment. A nine-Test triangular tournament involving England, South Africa and Australia was set up. The series was hampered by a very wet summer and player disputes however and the tournament was considered a failure with the Daily Telegraph stating:

Nine Tests provide a surfeit of cricket, and contests between Australia and South Africa are not a great attraction to the British public.With Australia sending a weakened team and the South African bowlers being ineffective England dominated the tournament winning four of their six matches. The match between Australia and South Africa at Lord's was visited by King George V, the first time a reigning monarch had watched Test cricket. England went on one more tour before the outbreak of the First World War, beating South Africa 4–0, with Barnes taking 49 wickets in the series.

- 1920s

England's first match after the war was in the 1920–21 season against Australia. Still feeling the effects of the war England went down to a series of crushing defeats and suffered their first whitewash losing the series 5–0. Six Australians scored hundreds while Mailey spun out 36 English batsmen. Things were no better in the next few Ashes series losing the 1921 Ashes series 3–0 and the 1924–25 Ashes 4–1. England's fortunes were to change in 1926 as they regained the Ashes and were a formidable team during this period dispatching Australia 4–1 in the 1928–29 Ashes tour.

On the same year the West Indies became the fourth nation to be granted Test status and played their first game against England. England won each of these three Tests by an innings, and a view was expressed in the press that their elevation had proved a mistake although Learie Constantine did the double on the tour. In the 1929–30 season England went on two concurrent tours with one team going to New Zealand (who were granted Test status earlier that year) and the other to the West Indies. Despite sending two separate teams England won both tours beating New Zealand 1–0 and the West Indies 2–1.

- 1930s

The 1930 Ashes series saw a young Don Bradman dominate the tour, scoring 974 runs in his seven Test innings. He scored 254 at Lord's, 334 at Headingley and 232 at The Oval. Australia regained the Ashes winning the series 3–1. As a result of Bradman's prolific run-scoring the England captain Douglas Jardine chose to develop the already existing leg theory into fast leg theory, or bodyline, as a tactic to stop Bradman. Fast leg theory involved bowling fast balls directly at the batsman's body. The batsman would need to defend himself, and if he touched the ball with the bat, he risked being caught by one of a large number of fielders placed on the leg side.

English cricket team at the Test match held at the Brisbane Exhibition Ground. England won the match by a record margin of 675 runs.Using Jardine's fast leg theory, England won the next Ashes series 4–1, but complaints about the Bodyline tactic caused crowd disruption on the tour, and threats of diplomatic action from the Australian Cricket Board, which during the tour sent the following cable to the MCC in London:

Bodyline bowling assumed such proportions as to menace best interests of game, making protection of body by batsmen the main consideration. Causing intensely bitter feeling between players as well as injury. In our opinion is unsportsmanlike. Unless stopped at once likely to upset friendly relations existing between Australia and England.

Later, Jardine was removed from the captaincy and the Laws of Cricket changed so that no more than one fast ball aimed at the body was permitted per over, and having more than two fielders behind square leg was banned.

England's following tour of India in the 1933–34 season was the first Test match to be staged in the subcontinent. The series was also notable for Stan Nichols and Nobby Clark bowling so many bouncers that the Indian batsman wore solar toupées instead of caps to protect themselves.

Australia won the 1934 Ashes series 2–1 and kept the urn for the following 19 years. Many of the wickets of the time were friendly to batsmen resulting in a large proportion of matches ending in high scoring draws and many batting records being set.

England drew the 1938 Ashes, meaning Australia retained the urn. England went into the final match of the series at The Oval 1–0 down, but won the final game by an innings and 579 runs. Len Hutton made the highest ever Test score by an Englishman, making 364 in England first innings to help them reach 903, their highest ever score against Australia.

The 1938–39 tour of South Africa saw another experiment with the deciding Test being a timeless Test that was played to a finish. England lead 1–0 going into the final timeless match at Durban. Despite the final Test being 'timeless', the game ended in a draw after 10 days as England had to catch the train to catch the boat home. A record 1,981 runs were scored, and the concept of timeless Tests was abandoned. England went on one final tour of the West Indies in 1939 before the Second World War, although a team for an MCC tour of India was selected more in hope than expectation of the matches being played.

- 1940s

Test cricket resumed after the war in 1946, and England won their first match back against India. However, they struggled in the 1946–47 Ashes series, losing 3–0 in Australia under Wally Hammond's captaincy. England beat South Africa 3–0 in 1947 with Denis Compton scoring 1,187 runs in the series.

The 1947–48 series against the West Indies was another disappointment for England, with the side losing 2–0 following injuries to several key players. England suffered further humiliation against Bradman's invincible side in the 1948 Ashes series. Hutton was controversially dropped for the third Test, and England were bowled out for just 52 at The Oval. The series proved to be Bradman's final Ashes series.

In 1948–49, England beat South Africa 2–0 under the captaincy of George Mann. The series included a record breaking stand of 359 between Hutton and Cyril Washbrook. The decade ended with England drawing the Test series against New Zealand, with every match ending in a draw.

- 1950s

Their fortunes changed on the 1953 Ashes tour as they won the series 1–0. England did not lose a series between their 1950–51 and 1958–59 tours of Australia and secured famous victory in 1954–55 under the captaincy of Len Hutton, thanks to Frank Tyson whose 6/85 at Sydney and 7/27 at Melbourne are remembered as the fastest bowling ever seen in Australia. The 1956 series was remembered for the bowling of Jim Laker who took 46 wickets at an average of 9.62, including figures of 19/90 at Old Trafford. After drawing to South Africa, England defeated the West Indies and New Zealand comfortably.

The England team then left for Australia in the 1958–59 season with a team that had been hailed as the strongest ever to leave on an Ashes tour but lost the series 4–0 as Richie Benaud's revitalised Australians were too strong, with England struggling with the bat throughout the series.

On 24 August 1959, England inflicted its only 5–0 whitewash over India. All out for 194 at The Oval, India lost the last test by an innings. England's batsman Ken Barrington and Colin Cowdrey both had an excellent series with the bat, with Barrington scoring 357 runs across the series and Cowdrey scoring 344.

- 1960s

The early and middle 1960s were poor periods for English cricket. Despite England's strength on paper, Australia held the Ashes and the West Indies dominated England in the early part of the decade. May stood down as captain in 1961 following the 1961 Ashes defeat.

Ted Dexter succeeded him as captain but England continued to suffer indifferent results. In 1961–62, they beat Pakistan, but also lost to India. The following year saw England and Australia tie the 1962–63 Ashes series 1–1, meaning Australia retained the urn. Despite beating New Zealand 3–0, England went on to lose to the West Indies, and again failed in the 1964 Ashes, losing the home series 1–0, which marked the end of Dexter's captaincy.

However, from 1968 to 1971 they played 27 consecutive Test matches without defeat, winning 9 and drawing 18 (including the abandoned Test at Melbourne in 1970–71). The sequence began when they drew with Australia at Lord's in the Second Test of the 1968 Ashes series and ended in 1971 when India won the Third Test at The Oval by four wickets. They played 13 Tests with only one defeat immediately beforehand and so played a total of 40 consecutive Tests with only one defeat, dating from their innings victory over the West Indies at The Oval in 1966. During this period they beat New Zealand, India, the West Indies, and Pakistan, and under Ray Illingworth's leadership, regained The Ashes from Australia in 1970–71.

- 1970s

The 1970s, for the England team, can be largely split into three parts. Early in the decade, Illingworth's side dominated world cricket, winning the Ashes away in 1971 and then retaining them at home in 1972. The same side beat Pakistan at home in 1971 and played by far the better cricket against India that season. However, England were largely helped by the rain to sneak the Pakistan series 1–0 but the same rain saved India twice and one England collapse saw them lose to India. This was, however, one of (if not the) strongest England team ever with the likes of Illingworth, Geoffrey Boycott, John Edrich, Basil D'Oliveira, Dennis Amiss, Alan Knott, John Snow and Derek Underwood at its core.

The mid-1970s were more turbulent. Illingworth and several others had refused to tour India in 1972–73 which led to a clamour for Illingworth's job by the end of that summer – England had just been beaten 2–0 by a flamboyant West Indies side – with several England players well over 35. Mike Denness was the surprising choice but only lasted 18 months; his results against poor opposition were good, but England were badly exposed as ageing and lacking in good fast bowling against the 1974–75 Australians, losing that series 4–1 to lose the Ashes.

Denness was replaced in 1975 by Tony Greig. While he managed to avoid losing to Australia, his side were largely thrashed the following year by the young and very much upcoming West Indies for whom Greig's infamous "grovel" remark acted as motivation. Greig's finest hour was probably the 1976–77 win over India in India. When Greig was discovered as being instrumental in World Series Cricket, he was sacked, and replaced by Mike Brearley.

Brearley's side showed again the hyperbole that is often spoken when one side dominates in cricket. While his side of 1977–80 contained some young players who went on to become England greats, most notably future captains Ian Botham, David Gower and Graham Gooch, their opponents were often very much weakened by the absence of their World Series players, especially in 1978, when England beat New Zealand 3–0 and Pakistan 2–0 before thrashing what was effectively Australia's 2nd XI 5–1 in 1978–79.

- 1980s

The England team, with Brearley's exit in 1980, was never truly settled throughout the 1980s, which will probably be remembered as a low point for the team. While some of the great players like Botham, Gooch and Gower had fine careers, the team seldom succeeded in beating good opposition throughout the decade and did not score a home Test victory between September 1985 and July 1990.

Botham took over the captaincy in 1980 and they put up a good fight against the West Indies, losing a five match Test series 1–0, although England were humbled in the return series. After scoring a pair in the first Test against Australia, Botham lost the captaincy due to his poor form, and was replaced by Brearley. Botham returned to form and played exceptionally in the remainder of the series, being named man of the match in the third, fourth and fifth Tests. The series became known as Botham's Ashes as England recorded a 3–1 victory.

Keith Fletcher took over as captain in 1981, but England lost his first series in charge against India. Bob Willis took over as captain in 1982 and enjoyed victories over India and Pakistan, but lost the Ashes after Australia clinched the series 2–1. England hosted the World Cup in 1983 and reached the semi-finals, but their Test form remained poor, as they suffered defeats against New Zealand, Pakistan and the West Indies.

Gower took over as skipper in 1984 and led the team to a 2–1 victory over India. They went on to win the 1985 Ashes 3–1, although after this came a poor run of form. Defeat to the West Indies dented the team's confidence, and they went on to lose to India 2–0. In 1986, Micky Stewart was appointed the first full-time England coach. England beat New Zealand, but there was little hope of them retaining the Ashes in 1986–87. However, despite being described as a team that 'can't bat, can't bowl and can't field', they went on to win the series 2–1.

After losing consecutive series against Pakistan, England drew a three match Test series against New Zealand 0–0. They reached the final of the 1987 World Cup, but lost by seven runs against Australia. After losing 4–0 to the West Indies, England lost the Ashes to a resurgent Australia led by Allan Border. With the likes of Gooch banned following a rebel tour to South Africa, a new look England side suffered defeat again against the West Indies, although this time by a margin of 2–1.

- 1990s

If the 1980s were a low point for English Test cricket, then the 1990s were only a slight improvement. The arrival of Gooch as captain in 1990 forced a move toward more professionalism and especially fitness though it took some time for old habits to die. Even in 2011, one or two successful county players have been shown up as physically unfit for international cricket. Creditable performances against India and New Zealand in 1990 were followed by a hard-fought draw against the 1991 West Indies and a strong performance in the 1992 Cricket World Cup in which the England team finished as runners-up for the second consecutive World Cup, but landmark losses against Australia in 1990–91 and especially Pakistan in 1992 showed England up badly in terms of bowling. So bad was England's bowling in 1993 that Rod Marsh described England's pace attack at one point as "pie throwers". Having lost three of the first four Tests played in England in 1993, Gooch resigned to be replaced by Michael Atherton.

More selectorial problems abounded during Atherton's reign as new chairman of selectors and coach Ray Illingworth (then into his 60s) assumed almost sole responsibility for the team off the field. The youth policy which had seen England emerge from the West Indies tour of 1993–94 with some credit (though losing to a seasoned Windies team) was abandoned and players such as Gatting and Gooch were persisted with when well into their 30s and 40s. England continued to do well at home against weaker opponents such as India, New Zealand and a West Indies side beginning to fade but struggled badly against improving sides like Pakistan and South Africa.

Atherton had offered his resignation after losing the 1997 Ashes series 3–2 having been 1–0 up after two matches – eventually to resign one series later in early 1998. England, looking for talent, went through a whole raft of new players during this period, such as Ronnie Irani, Adam Hollioake, Craig White, Graeme Hick and Mark Ramprakash. At this time, there were two main problems:The lack of a genuine all-rounder to bat at 6, Botham having left a huge gap in the batting order when he retired from Tests in 1992.

Alec Stewart, a sound wicket-keeper and an excellent player of quick bowling, could not open and keep wicket, hence his batting down the order, where he was often exposed to spin which he did not play as well.

Stewart took the reins as captain in 1998, but another losing Ashes series and early World Cup exit cost him Test and ODI captaincy in 1999. This should not detract from the 1998 home Test series where England showed great fortitude to beat a powerful South African side 2–1.

Another reason for their poor performances were the demands of County Cricket teams on their players, meaning that England could rarely field a full-strength team on their tours. This eventually led to the ECB taking over from the MCC as the governing body of England and the implementation of central contracts. 1992 also saw Scotland sever ties with the England and Wales team, and begin to compete as the Scotland national team.

By 1999, with coach David Lloyd resigning after the World Cup exit and new captain Nasser Hussain just appointed, England hit rock bottom after losing 2–1 to New Zealand in shambolic fashion. Hussain was booed on the Oval balcony as the crowd jeered "We’ve got the worst team in the world" to the tune of "He’s Got the Whole World in His Hands".

- 2000s

Central contracts were installed – reducing players workloads – and following the arrival of Zimbabwean coach Duncan Fletcher, England thrashed the fallen West Indies 3–1. England’s results in Asia improved that winter with series wins against both Pakistan and Sri Lanka. Hussain’s side had a far harder edge to it, avoiding the anticipated "Greenwash" in the 2001

Ashes series against the all-powerful Australian team. The nucleus the side was slowly coming together as players such as Hussain himself, Graham Thorpe, Darren Gough and Ashley Giles began to be regularly selected. By 2003 though, having endured another Ashes drubbing as well as another first-round exit from the World Cup, Hussain resigned as captain after one Test against South Africa.

Michael Vaughan took over, with players encouraged to express themselves. England won five consecutive Test series prior to facing Australia in the 2005 Ashes series, taking the team to second place in the ICC Test Championship table. During this period England defeated the West Indies home and away, New Zealand, and Bangladesh at home, and South Africa in South Africa. In June 2005, England played its first ever T20 international match, defeating Australia by 100 runs. Later that year, England defeated Australia 2–1 in a thrilling series to regain the Ashes for the first time in 16 years, having lost them in 1989. Following the 2005 Ashes win, the team suffered from a spate of serious injuries to key players such as Vaughan, Giles, Andrew Flintoff and Simon Jones. As a result, the team underwent an enforced period of transition. A 2–0 defeat in Pakistan was followed by two drawn away series with India and Sri Lanka.

In the home Test series victory against Pakistan in July and August 2006, several promising new players emerged. Most notable were the left-arm orthodox spin bowler Monty Panesar, the first Sikh to play Test cricket for England, and left-handed opening batsman Alastair Cook. The 2006–07 Ashes series was keenly anticipated and was expected to provide a level of competition comparable to the 2005 series. In the event, England, captained by Flintoff who was deputising for the injured Vaughan, lost all five Tests to concede the first Ashes whitewash in 86 years.

In the 2007 Cricket World Cup, England lost to most of the Test playing nations they faced, beating only the West Indies and Bangladesh, although they also avoided defeat by any of the non-Test playing nations. Even so, the unimpressive nature of most of their victories in the tournament, combined with heavy defeats by New Zealand, Australia and South Africa, left many commentators criticising the manner in which the England team approached the one-day game. Coach Duncan Fletcher resigned after eight years in the job as a result and was succeeded by former Sussex coach Peter Moores.

In 2007–08, England toured Sri Lanka and New Zealand, losing the first series 1–0 and winning the second 2–1. These series were followed up at home in May 2008 with a 2–0 home series win against New Zealand, with the results easing pressure on Moores – who was not at ease with his team, particularly star batsman Kevin Pietersen. Pietersen succeeded Vaughan as captain in June 2008, after England had been well beaten by South Africa at home. The poor relationship between the two came to a head on the 2008–09 tour to India. England lost the series 1–0 and both men resigned their positions, although Pietersen remained a member of the England team. Moores was replaced as coach by Zimbabwean Andy Flower. Against this background, England toured the West Indies under the captaincy of Andrew Strauss and, in a disappointing performance, lost the Test series 1–0.

The 2009 Ashes series featured the first Test match played in Wales, at Sophia Gardens, Cardiff. England drew the match thanks to a last-wicket stand by bowlers James Anderson and Panesar. A victory for each team followed before the series was decided at The Oval. Thanks to fine bowling by Stuart Broad and Graeme Swann and a debut century by Jonathan Trott, England regained the Ashes.

- 2010s

After a drawn Test series in South Africa, England won their first ever ICC world championship, the 2010 World Twenty20, with a seven-wicket win over Australia in Barbados. The following winter in the 2010–11 Ashes, they beat Australia 3–1 to retain the urn and record their first series win in Australia for 24 years. Furthermore, all three of their wins were by an innings – the first time a touring side had ever recorded three innings victories in a single Test series. Cook earned Man of the Series with 766 runs.

England struggled to match their Test form in the 2011 Cricket World Cup. Despite beating South Africa and tying with eventual winners India, England suffered shock losses to Ireland and Bangladesh before losing in the quarter-finals to Sri Lanka.However the team's excellent form in the Test match arena continued and on 13 August 2011, they became the world's top-ranked Test team after comfortably whitewashing India 4–0, their sixth consecutive series victory and eighth in the past nine series. However, this status only lasted a year – having lost 3–0 to Pakistan over the winter, England were beaten 2–0 by South Africa, who replaced them at the top of the rankings. It was their first home series loss since 2008, against the same opposition.

This loss saw the resignation of Strauss as captain (and his retirement from cricket). Cook, who was already in charge of the ODI side, replaced Strauss and led England to a 2–1 victory in India – their first in the country since 1984–85. In doing so, he became the first captain to score centuries in his first five Tests as captain and became England's leading century-maker with 23 centuries to his name.

- The England team celebrate victory over Australia in the 2015 Ashes series

After finishing as runners-up in the ICC Champions Trophy, England faced Australia in back-to-back Ashes series. A 3–0 home win secured England the urn for the fourth time in five series. However, in the return series, they found themselves utterly demolished in a 5–0 defeat, their second Ashes whitewash in under a decade. Their misery was compounded by batsman Jonathan Trott leaving the tour early due to a stress-related illness and the mid-series retirement of spinner Graeme Swann. Following the tour, head coach Flower resigned his post while Pietersen was dropped indefinitely from the England team.

Flower was replaced by his predecessor, Moores, but he was sacked for a second time after a string of disappointing results including failing to advance from the group stage at the 2015 World Cup. He was replaced by Australian Trevor Bayliss who oversaw an upturn of form in the ODI side, including series victories against New Zealand and Pakistan. In the Test arena, England reclaimed the Ashes 3–2 in the summer of 2015.

England entered the 2019 Cricket World Cup as favourites, having been ranked the number one ODI side by the ICC for over a year prior to the tournament. However, shock defeats to Pakistan and Sri Lanka during the group stage left them on the brink of elimination and needing to win their final two games against India and New Zealand to guarantee progression to the semi-finals. This was achieved, putting their campaign back on track, and an eight-wicket victory over Australia in the semi-final at Edgbaston meant England were in their first World Cup final since 1992. The final against New Zealand at Lord's has been described as one of the greatest and most dramatic matches in the history of cricket, with some calling it the "greatest ODI in history", as both the match and subsequent Super Over were tied, after England went into the final over of their innings 14 runs behind New Zealand's total. England won by virtue of having scored more boundaries throughout the match, securing their maiden World Cup title in their fourth final appearance.

- England and Wales Cricket Board

The England and Wales Cricket Board (ECB) is the governing body of English cricket and the England cricket team. The Board has been operating since 1 January 1997 and represents England on the International Cricket Council. The ECB is also responsible for the generation of income from the sale of tickets, sponsorship and broadcasting rights, primarily in relation to the England team. The ECB's income in the 2006 calendar year was £77 million.

Prior to 1997, the Test and County Cricket Board (TCCB) was the governing body for the English team. Apart from in Test matches, when touring abroad, the England team officially played as MCC up to and including the 1976–77 tour of Australia, reflecting the time when MCC had been responsible for selecting the touring party. The last time the England touring team wore the bacon-and-egg colours of the MCC was on the 1996–97 tour of New Zealand.

- Status of Wales

Historically, the England team represented the whole of Great Britain in international cricket, with Scottish or Welsh national teams playing sporadically and players from both countries occasionally representing England. Scotland became an independent member of the ICC in 1994, having severed links with the TCCB two years earlier.

Criticism has been made of the England and Wales Cricket Board using only the England name while utilising Welsh players such as Simon and Geraint Jones. With Welsh players pursuing international careers exclusively with an England team, there have been a number of calls for Wales to become an independent member of the ICC, or for the ECB to provide more fixtures for a Welsh national team.However, both Cricket Wales and Glamorgan County Cricket Club have continually supported the ECB, with Glamorgan arguing for the financial benefits of the Welsh county within the English structure, and Cricket Wales stating they are "committed to continuing to play a major role within the ECB".

The absence of a Welsh cricket team has seen a number of debates within the Welsh Senedd. In 2013 a debate saw both Conservative and Labour members lend their support to the establishment of an independent Welsh team.

In 2015, a report produced by the Welsh National Assembly's petitions committee, reflected the passionate debate around the issue. Bethan Jenkins, Plaid Cymru's spokesperson on heritage, culture, sport and broadcasting, and a member of the petitions committee, argued that Wales should have its own international team and withdraw from the ECB. Jenkins noted that Ireland (with a population of 6.4 million) was an ICC member with 6,000 club players whereas Wales (with 3 million) had 7,500. Jenkins said: "Cricket Wales and Glamorgan CCC say the idea of a Welsh national cricket team is 'an emotive subject', of course having a national team is emotive, you only have to look at the stands during any national game to see that. To suggest this as anything other than natural is a bit of a misleading argument."

In 2017, the First Minister of Wales, Carwyn Jones called for the reintroduction of the Welsh one-day team stating: "[It] is odd that we see Ireland and Scotland playing in international tournaments and not Wales."

- England at 2021

In February 2021, England and Wales Cricket Board announced that England's Principal partner NatWest has been replaced by Cinch, an online used car marketplace. England's kit is manufactured by New Balance, who replaced previous manufacturer Adidas in April 2017.

When playing Test cricket, England's cricket whites feature the three lions badge on the left of the shirt and the name of the sponsor Cinch on the centre. English fielders may wear a navy blue cap or white sun hat with the ECB logo in the middle. Helmets are also coloured navy blue. Before 1997 the uniform sported the TCCB lion and stumps logo on the uniforms, while the helmets, jumpers and hats had the three lions emblem.

In limited overs cricket, England's ODI and Twenty20 shirts feature the Cinch logo across the centre, with the three lions badge on the left of the shirt and the New Balance logo on the right. In ODIs, the kit comprises a blue shirt with navy trousers, whilst the Twenty20 kit comprises a flame red shirt and navy trousers. In ICC limited-overs tournaments, a modified kit design is used with sponsor's logo moving to the sleeve and 'ENGLAND' printed across the front.

Over the years, England's ODI kit has cycled between various shades of blue (such as a pale blue used until the mid-1990s, when it was replaced in favour of a bright blue) with the occasional all-red kit.In April 2017, ECB brought back traditional cable-knit sweater for test matches under new supplier New Balance.

CHAPTER THREE

History of the England cricket

- History of the England cricket

The history of the England cricket team can be said to date back to at least 1739, when sides styled "Kent" and "All England" played a match at Bromley Common. Over 300 matches involving "England" or "All England" prior to 1877 are known. However these teams were usually put together on an ad hoc basis and were rarely fully representative.

The history of the current England side can be traced to 1877 when England played in what was subsequently recognised as the very first Test match. Since then, up to 20 August 2006 they have played 852 Test matches, winning 298, losing 245 and drawing 309. During these 852 matches, they have been captained by 77 different players.

- Early history

The term "All-England" was first used in reports of two Kent v All-England matches in July 1739.

The first match was at Bromley Common in Kent on Monday 9 July 1739. It was billed as between "eleven gentlemen of that county (i.e., Kent) and eleven gentlemen from any part of England, exclusive of Kent". Kent, described as "the Unconquerable County" won by "a very few notches".

The second match was at the Artillery Ground in Bunhill Fields, Finsbury on Monday 23 July 1739. This game was drawn and a report includes the phrase "eleven picked out of all England".

In subsequent decades there were many more such matches between a side representing a county, or the MCC, and a side drawn from the rest of England and described as "England" or "All England". As the next section describes, in 1846 the term "All England Eleven" would acquire a new, more precise, definition.

- The All-England XI

In 1846 William Clarke formed the All-England Eleven as a touring team of leading players to play matches at big city venues, mainly in the North of England. Clarke's team was a top-class side worthy of its title. The AEE lasted until 1880. In 1852, several players set up the United All-England Eleven as a rival to the AEE, and from 1857 to 1866 the annual match between these two teams was arguably the most important contest of the English season – certainly judged by the quality of the players.

- The 1873/4 team.

The early overseas tours were organised as purely commercial ventures, as indeed were the first Test-playing tours. The first such tour was to North America by a team of English professionals, departing England in September 1859. The team comprised six players from the All-England Eleven and six from the United All-England Eleven, and was captained by George Parr. They played five matches, winning them all. There were no first-class fixtures.

With the outbreak of the American Civil War, attention turned to Australia. The inaugural tour of the country took place in 1861–2, and was organised by Messrs Spiers & Pond. Led by HH Stephenson, the English team played 12 matches, but none were first-class.

In 1863–4, the Melbourne Cricket Club organised a tour by an English team under the captaincy of George Parr, which also visited New Zealand. The team played 16 matches, but none were first-class.

There were further tours of North America (taking in both the US and Canada) in late 1868, led by Edgar Willsher, and in late 1872, under R.A. Fitzgerald. The latter side included W.G.Grace.

In 1873–4, the Melbourne Cricket Club organised a tour by a team under the captaincy of WG Grace, which played 15 matches, but none were first-class.

Most of the matches of these early touring teams were played "against odds", that is to say the opposing team was permitted to have more than eleven players (usually twenty-two) in order to make a more even contest.

- 1877 to 1890

James Lillywhite, a professional with Sussex CCC, led a team which had sailed on the P&O steamship Poonah on 21 September 1876. They played in Australia and then New Zealand before returning to Australia to play a combined Australian XI, for once on even terms of XI a side. The match, starting on 15 March 1877 at the Melbourne Cricket Ground, came to be regarded as the first Test match, although none of its participants could have guessed at its significance at the time. Charles Bannerman, of Australia, faced the first ball and scored the first century, a glorious 165 before retiring hurt with a broken finger. The next highest score in this inaugural Test for Australia was Tom Horan with 10. Alfred Shaw of England bowled the first ball and took 5 for 38 in Australia's second innings. Tom Kendall, born in England, took 7 English wickets for 55 to bring Australia victory by 45 runs. 100 years later, in the Centenary Test, the result and margin would be exactly the same. England won a second match to square the series.

In 1878/79 Kent captain and MCC luminary Lord Harris took a team, consisting mainly of amateurs, to Australia where they lost by 10 wickets at Melbourne. Their batting was reasonably strong but the lack of professional bowlers cost them dear. The tour became famous for an unseemly incident in a tour game at Sydney where a near riot broke out. One of the umpires was Edmund Barton, who became Australia's first prime minister.

The 1880 Australian tourists were the first to play a Test match on English soil. Their 'demon' bowler, Fred Spofforth, sustained a hand injury and, crucially, missed the game in which W.G. Grace scored 152 and Billy Murdoch one run better. Lord Harris led the victorious England side at the Oval.

An all professional side, organised by Shaw, Shrewsbury and Lillywhite sailed to Australia for the 1881/82 campaign. The tour was bedeviled with scandal and allegations of fisticuffs, betting and heavy drinking. Tom Garrett took 18 wickets in the three Tests played for Australia. Many of the tour matches were still against local '22's. Australia won the four Test series 2 – 0.

The developing rivalry took on a new turn in 1882, when England lost at home at The Oval in the solitary Test of the summer. Spofforth took 7 for 46 and 7 for 44 and Ted Peate, Yorkshire slow left armer who had taken 8 wickets, was out just 8 runs short of victory. Upset at this turn of events, The Sporting Times printed an obituary to English cricket: "In

Affectionate Remembrance of ENGLISH CRICKET, which died at the Oval on 29th AUGUST 1882, Deeply lamented by a large circle of sorrowing friends and acquaintances R.I.P. N.B. – The body will be cremated and the ashes taken to Australia."

When England toured Australia the following winter of 1882/83 and won 2–1, the England captain, the Hon. Ivo Bligh was presented with an urn that contained some ashes, which have variously been said to be of a bail, ball or even a woman's veil. And so The Ashes series was born. Yorkshire stalwart Billy Bates, who played all his 15 Tests on 5 tours to Australia, scored 55 and took 14 for 102 at Melbourne in the second Test, including the first Test hat-trick, to bring England the first innings victory in Test cricket. A.G. Steel made 135* at Sydney – although he did drop Bonner 4 times (out of 8 drops in total) as the giant Australian hitter scored 87.

England won 1–0 in the three Test series in 1884. Peate took 6 for 85 in Australia's first innings, and Ulyett 7 for 36, the second as England won by an innings Lord's where Steel made a wonderful 148 out of England's first innings of 379. Australia's captain Billy Murdoch scored the first Test double hundred at the Oval where Walter Read of England hit a century in 113 minutes after going in at number 10. All 11 Englishmen bowled in Australia's innings, including wicket keeper Lyttelton with underarm lobs.

England embarked on a long stretch of dominance. They won 14 and lost only 3 of the Tests played between 1884 and 1890. Billy Barnes hit 134 in the opening Adelaide Test of the five Test 1884/85 series while Johnny Briggs of Lancashire hit a two-hour ton at Melbourne in the second, where Australia fielded a completely new team of 11 different players after a dispute over gate money. Wilfred Flowers scored 56 and took 5 for 46 in the third Test at Sydney where Australia pulled back a game thanks to Bonner smashing a century in even time. England won the deciding fifth Test by an innings at Melbourne, Arthur Shrewsbury making 105*.

W. G. Grace scored 170 in the Oval Test of 1886, beating the individual Test innings record of 164 set by Arthur Shrewsbury in the previous match on an evil pitch at Lords. England won by an innings on the third day after Australia were bowled out for 68 and 149m with George Lohmann of Surrey taking 12 for 104. The Australian tourists, without Bannerman or Murdoch and often losing Spofforth to injuries, lost all three Tests.

Shrewsbury's England beat Australia in both matches on the 1886–87 tour, despite being bowled out for 45 on the first day at Sydney. Two England parties toured there in 1887–88, with Shaw and Shrewsbury's team sponsored by Melbourne CC and Lord Harris's team by the Sydney Association. The two sides joined up for one Test Match at Sydney which they won thanks to Lohmann's 9 wickets and Bobby Peel's 10. Australia made just 42 and 82 on a poor pitch in bad light.

The 1888 Australians won at Lords but lost at The Oval and Old Trafford. Their bowling was penetrative, particularly Jack Ferris and the 'terror' Charlie Turner, but their batting was too weak to withstand the English professionals in their home conditions. Bobby Peel took 11 wickets at Old Trafford.

England won the first Test in South Africa, at Port Elizabeth in March 1889 by 8 wickets, despite fielding a less than first choice XI. W.H. Ashley took 7 for 95 for South Africa in his only Test. Bobby Abel of Surrey scored 120 for England in the Second Test, the first hundred scored in South Africa. Bernard Tancred of South Africa became the first Test batsman to carry his bat, for 26*, as South Africa collapsed to 47 all out. M.P. Bowden remains the youngest man to captain England, at just 23 years and 144 days. Johnny Briggs took 7 for 17 and 8 for 11 at Cape Town, 14 bowled and 1 LBW.

- 1890s

Four ball overs gave way to five ball overs in the 1890s and to six ball overs in Australia, as the game continued to develop quickly. England won the 1890 Ashes series 2–0, although Jack Barrett carried his bat for 67 through Australia's second innings of 176 at Lord's. W. G. Grace was out second ball in the first innings but saw England home in the second with 75*. Frederick Martin took 12 Australian wickets for 102 but 'Nutty' never played an Ashes match again. The third scheduled match, at Old Trafford, was the first Test to be abandoned without a ball being bowled.

W. G. Grace's tourists lost 2–1 on the 1891–92 tour, Australia winning at Melbourne and Sydney, where Bannerman batted for seven and a half hours and scored only three boundaries and England's Bobby Abel carried his bat for 132. England claimed a consolation innings victory at Adelaide where Stoddard scored 134 and Peel 83 and Briggs took 6 wickets in each innings.

England won the only Test on the 1891/92 tour of South Africa at Cape Town, where Harry Wood, the Surrey wicket keeper made 134 not out and Ferris, who had earlier played for Australia, took 13 for 91. Billy Murdoch was another Australian turned Englishman on the tour.

- England regained the Ashes in 1893, with an innings win at The Oval and draws in the other two Tests. W. G. Grace and A.E. Stoddart made three consecutive century opening stands. William Gunn of Nottinghamshire scored his only Test hundred, 102*, at Old Trafford, while Arthur Shrewsbury scored 106 at Lord's. Future England great Ranjitsinhji was one of the unfortunate bowlers as Australia set a new record team score of 843 against 'Oxford and Cambridge Past and Present' in Portsmouth.

Andrew Stoddart led England to a thrilling 3–2 victory on the 1894–1895 Ashes tour. Bobby Peel took the final wickets in the first Test victory at Sydney and the second at Melbourne and hit the winning runs in the final and deciding Test at the MCG. England's amazing victory at Sydney, by 10 runs, came after they had followed on with Lancashire's Albert Ward hitting 75 and 117 in the game. J.T. Brown scored 140 for England at Melbourne where England were set 297 to win. He reached 50 in 28 minutes and put on a then record 210 with Ward as England won by six wickets. Tom Richardson took 32 wickets in the Tests.

- England won all three Tests of the 1895/96 tour of South Africa by resounding margins. Lohmann was unplayable, taking 7 for 38 and 8 for 7 at Port Elizabeth and finishing with a hat trick. He took 9 for 28 and 3 for 43 at Johannesburg and 7 for 42 and 1 for 45 at Cape Town.

Having been overlooked for the first Test at Lord's, where Australian captain Harry Trott scored 143 and put on a record 210 with Syd Gregory (103), Shri Ranjitsinhji burst into Test cricket with 62 and 154 at Old Trafford in 1896. His magical batting and Tom Richardson's 13 for 244 were not enough to prevent Australia running out winners by 3 wickets however. Five English professionals went on 'strike' for more money before the Oval Test. Abel, Hayward and Richardson relented, but Gunn and Lohmann never played for England again. England won the series 2–1.

The Ashes were lost on Andrew Stoddart's 1897/98 tour, with Australia thumping England 4–1. Australian Joe Darling was the first batsmen to make 500 runs in a Test series, including 101 at Sydney, 178 at Adelaide and 160 in the final Sydney Test, where his hundred came up in 91 minutes. Stoddart's mother died just before the first Test and he was too distraught to play in either of the first two matches. Ranji, batting at number 7 after a throat infection, scored a brilliant 175 in the first Test and took England over 500 for the first time in a game won by 9 wickets but the Englishmen lost the next four heavily.

Lord Hawke's tourists in 1898/99 played and won two Tests in South Africa, with sometime Australian Albert Trott taking 17 wickets. Plum Warner carried his bat for 132 at Johannesburg in his maiden Test.

The 1899 series against Australia saw two significant developments. For the first time in England, five Tests were played rather than three, with Trent Bridge and Headingley being added to the "traditional" venues of Lord's, The Oval and Old Trafford. Also MCC and the counties appointed a selection committee for the first time. It comprised three active players: Lord Hawke, W.G. Grace and H.W. Bainbridge who was the captain of Warwickshire. Prior to this, England teams for home Tests had been chosen by the club on whose ground the match was to be played. The peerless Australian Victor Trumper dominated the series. He scored 1,500 runs on the tour, including 300 not out against Sussex and a breathtaking century in Australia's sole, but deciding, Test victory at Lords. W.G. Grace played his last Test at Trent Bridge. F.S. Jackson and Tom Hayward put on 185 at the Oval for the first wicket. England, scoring 576, forced Australia (352) to follow on, but the Australians played out the draw and with it retained the Ashes.

- 1900–1914: The "Golden Age"

The first Test series of the new century took place in Australia 1901–1902 and was won by Australia who came from one down to take the series 4–1. The England side was a private venture of Archie MacLaren (although the matches were all official Test matches). It was rather an attritional series of matches with only three centuries being scored and only one team innings over 400 (the first innings of England in the First Test at the SCG). Sydney Barnes made his debut for England and took 19 wickets in the first two Tests before being injured in the third and talking no further part in the series.

There was a home series against Australia in 1902 which was won by the Australians (2–1). In the drawn First Test at Edgbaston Australia were dismissed for 36 in their first innings (Wilfred Rhodes 7 for 17) but rain meant that the match was drawn. Rain also ruined the following match at Lord's. Sydney Barnes returned to the England team and had immediate success, taking seven wickets in the third Test at Sheffield (the only Test ever to be played there).

However England still lost the match. The final two Tests were amongst the most exciting of all time. A brilliant century by Trumper helped Australia to win the match at Old Trafford by three runs. England's batting throughout the series was modest with only one innings of over 300 and with only three centuries scored. The last of these was a match-winning innings in the final Test at The Oval by Gilbert Jessop, who went in at number seven in the second innings with England 48–5 and scored what was then the fastest century in Test cricket in 70 minutes, setting up an improbable England win by one wicket. The last wicket pair of Wilfred Rhodes and George Hirst nervelessly acquired the final fifteen runs needed for victory.

England toured Australia in 1903–1904, the first time that the MCC had been responsible for an England tour overseas. England regained The Ashes with a 3–2 series win under the captaincy of Plum Warner. In the first Test R.E.Foster made his Test debut and scored 287 in his first ever innings – the then highest ever Test score and a record that was to stand for a quarter of a century. Wilfred Rhodes took 15 wickets in England's second Test win at the MCG –a record that was to stand for thirty years. In the fifth Test England were dismissed for 61 in their first innings on a rain-affected pitch.

In 1905 Australia toured England and were beaten 2–0 with three matches drawn. Notable batting performances in the series included centuries by A.C. MacLaren, F.S. Jackson (2), Johnny Tyldesley (2) and C.B. Fry. B.J.T. Bosanquet, the inventor of the googly, took eight wickets in an Innings in the First Test.

In 1905–06 Plum Warner took an MCC team to South Africa for the first time and England were soundly beaten 4–1 in the series. England's batting faltered throughout the series with only one team innings in excess of 200 (successive innings of 184,190,148,160,295,196,198,160,187 and 130) and just one individual century (by F.L.Fane in the 3rd Test at the Wanderers). England's only win came at Newlands where the left-arm slow bowler Colin Blythe took eleven wickets in the match.

In 1907 there was a home three match Test series against South Africa which England, captained by R.E.Foster, won 1–0. Highlights included another sparkling innings by Gilbert Jessop who scored 93 at Lord's in a partnership of 145 for the sixth wicket with Len Braund who scored a century. There was another fine bowling performance by Blythe, who took 15 wickets at Headingley on a rain-affected match in a match that England won despite having been bowled out for 76 in their first innings.

In England's Test series in Australia in 1907–08 Australia won the first Test but England hit back well with a narrow win at the MCG in the 2nd Test in which Jack Hobbs made his England debut scoring 83 and 28. England were outplayed by Australia in the next three Tests and lost the series and the Ashes 4–1. England's batting was fragile throughout the series with only Gunn (2) and Hutchings scoring hundreds. The bowling relied on Jack Crawford), Arthur Fielder and Barnes, who took 79 wickets between them.

In a home series against Australia in 1909 England lost 2–1 (two draws) and no combination of players (England used 25 in total in the series) seemed to work. England failed to make 200 in an innings five times and there was only one individual century (by J. Sharp in the 3rd Test). The remarkable Colin Blythe delivered England's only victory by taking eleven wickets in the First Test at Edgbaston, but thereafter Australia, whilst never dominating the England attack, always had the edge.

England returned to South Africa in 1909–10 under H.D.G. Leveson-Gower, for a five match Test series and fared little better than on their first visit in 1905–06. The series was lost 3–2 but this disguises South Africa's superiority. The main highlight was Jack Hobbs first (of 15) Test century in the final Test at Newlands, he put on a then record 211 for the first wicket with Wilfred Rhodes. This was one of only two personal hundreds by England batsmen in the series. The bowling attack was weak – although the last of the great "lob" (underhand) bowlers George Simpson-Hayward had field days in the first three Test matches when he took a total of 21 wickets. Colin Blythe bowled England to a consolation win in the fifth Test with ten wickets in the match. Legspin dominated on the matting pitches, with the ball often bouncing chest high. Vogler took 29 wickets for the home side and Faulkner 29.

England toured Australia in 1911/12 under Plum Warner, but Johnny Douglas took over the captaincy when Warner fell ill prior to the first Test. Despite losing that first match at Sydney, a side which boasted Jack Hobbs, Frank Woolley, Sydney Barnes and Wilfred Rhodes hit back to take the next four Tests in style. Frank Foster and Barnes dominated with the ball, sharing 66 wickets, while Hobbs, Rhodes and Woolley recorded centuries. Hobbs and Rhodes shared opening stands of 147 at Adelaide and a then record 323 at Melbourne in the next Test where Barnes dismissed Bardsley, Kelleway, Hill and Armstrong for 3 runs in his opening spell. Later in the game, when the crowd barracked Barnes for deliberating over a field setting, he threw the ball down in disgust and refused to continue until order was restored. Frank Woolley also hit 305* in 205 minutes in a tour game against Tasmania.

The 1912 home season saw a unique experiment with a 9 Test triangular tournament involving South Africa and Australia but it was an idea ahead of its time and was not repeated. C.B. Fry of Sussex captained the team against Syd Gregory of Australia and Frank Mitchell of South Africa. Jack Hobbs scored 107 against Australia at Lords in a rain ruined game. The Australia v South Africa match, at Lord's, was notable for a visit by King George V, the first time a reigning monarch had watched Test cricket. Barnes took 34 wickets in his 3 Tests against the South Africans.

England's 1913/14 tour of South Africa was the last before the onset of World War I, and England dominated the rubber, winning 4–0. Syd Barnes was once again unplayable, taking 49 wickets in four Tests before boycotting the last in a row over his wife's accommodation. Only Herbie Taylor resisted for the home side, with skilful backfoot defence on the matting pitches, scoring 508 runs at 50.8.

- 1920s

England resumed their Test cricket after World War I with a tour of Australia in 1920/21 under Johnny Douglas. After the ravages of the war it was little surprise when England went down to a series of crushing defeats, the first 5–0 whitewash. Six Australians scored hundreds while Mailey spun out 36 English batsmen. Things were no better when Warwick Armstrong's men toured England in 1921. Australian fast bowlers Gregory and McDonald battered the English batsmen with a succession of bouncers and Jack Hobbs missed most of the season with first a leg injury then appendicitis. England used 30 players in all. Only one Australian made a century as opposed to 3 for England – A. C. "Jack" Russell scoring 101 and 102* and Phil Mead 182* – but Australia's 3–0 victory made it 8 Ashes defeats in succession.

England resumed the winning habit on the 1922/23 tour of South Africa, under F.T. Mann, winning a pulsating rubber 2 – 1. England lost the first Test but scraped to victory in the next, at Cape Town, by one wicket. Phil Mead scored 181 at Kingsmead, Durban, to ensure a draw and they won the fifth and final match, also at Durban, thanks to Jack Russell's twin centuries in his final Test. This dominance was underlined in England in 1924 with a 3–0 for England.

Hopes that the Ashes might be regained were dashed on the 1924/25 tour down under however, Australia thrashing England 4–1, although England scored 8 centuries to Australia's 6. Herbert Sutcliffe scored 734 runs at 81.56 and Maurice Tate broke Mailey's Ashes record with 38 wickets, bowling 2,528 balls in the Tests. England's only victory came at Melbourne, by an innings, after Captain Arthur Gilligan won the toss for the only time. It was England's first Ashes Test win in 12 years.

England drew the first four Tests of the 1926 Ashes series and so the series rested on the Oval Test, for which Percy Chapman replaced Arthur Carr as captain and both the 48-year-old Rhodes and 21-year-old Larwood were selected. Hobbs and Sutcliffe scored centuries and Australia lost by 289 runs. The South African team proved stronger than before however and drew the 1927/28 series 2–2.

A fourth team was, at last, introduced to Test cricket when the West Indies took their bow in 1928. England won each of the three Tests by an innings, Freeman taking 22 wickets, and a view was expressed in the press that their elevation had proved a mistake although 'electric heels' Learie Constantine did the double on the tour. The England team at this period was as strong as it has ever been and Australia were dispatched 4–1 on the 1928/29 Ashes tour. Hammond scored 44, 28, 251, 200, 32, 119*, 177, 38 and 16 – a total of 905 runs, a new record. Percy Chapman captained the team but barely played again.

England, under J. C. White and Arthur Carr, beat South Africa 2–0 at home in 1929 with Herbert Sutcliffe scoring a hundred in each innings at the Oval Bizarrely there were two concurrent England tours in 1929/30, one to New Zealand and one to the West Indies. Surrey paceman Maurice Allom took four wickets in five balls in New Zealand's maiden Test match, including a hat trick, and his 8 for 65 swept England to victory in Christchurch by 8 wickets with the three later Tests drawn. At the same time another England team were drawing 1–1 in the West Indies under F. S. G. Calthorpe. Forty-year-old Patsy Hendren made 1,765 runs on this tour and Andy Sandham scored 325 at Kingston (out of England's 849) in his final Test. The 'black Bradman' George Headley followed twin centuries at Georgetown with 223 in the same Kingston game.

- 1930s

The 21-year-old Don Bradman dominated the 1930 Ashes series in England, scoring 974 runs in his seven Test innings. He scored 254 at Lord's, 334 at Headingley, when Chapman stuck to attacking fields all day, and 232 at the Oval. Australia regained the Ashes. Harold Larwood took only four wickets in the series although K. S. Duleepsinhji made 173 at Lord's on debut.

England played five Tests in South Africa on the 1930/31 tour. Chasing 240 to win the first Test at the Old Wanderers ground in Johannesburg they were bowled out by E. P. Nupen, a master on the matting wicket, and drew the next four.

New Zealand played their first Test in England in 1931 and their strong performance at Lord's led the authorities to arrange another two that summer, one of which England won. India played their first Test in England in 1932 at Lords, reducing England to 19 for 3 on the first morning before losing a competitive match when they were bowled out for 187 chasing 346.

Bill Woodfull evades a Bodyline ball. Note the number of leg-side fielders.

Before the 1932–3 tour to Australia, England had become used to the prolific run-scoring of Don Bradman. The England captain, Surrey's Douglas Jardine chose to develop the already existing leg theory into fast leg theory, or bodyline, as a tactic to stop Bradman. Fast leg theory involved bowling fast balls directly at the batsman's body, and Jardine had two very fast accurate bowlers, Harold Larwood and Bill Voce to bowl them. The batsman would need to defend himself, and if he touched the ball with the bat, he risked being caught by one of a large number of fielders placed on the leg side.

England won the series and the Ashes 4–1. But complaints about the Bodyline tactic caused crowd disruption on the tour, and threats of diplomatic action from the Australian Cricket Board, which during the tour sent the following cable to the Marylebone Cricket Club in London:

Bodyline bowling assumed such proportions as to menace best interests of game, making protection of body by batsmen the main consideration. Causing intensely bitter feeling between players as well as injury. In our opinion is unsportsmanlike. Unless stopped at once likely to upset friendly relations existing between Australia and England.

Later, Jardine was removed from the captaincy and the laws of cricket changed so that no more than one fast ball aimed at the body was permitted per over, and having more than two fielders behind square leg were banned.

England won two Tests on the 1933/34 tour of India, the first ever Tests held in the sub continent. England won by nine wickets at Bombay's Gymkhana ground with Bryan Valentine scoring 136 in his first Test innings. Morris Nichols and E. W. "Nobby" Clark bowled so many bouncers at the Indian batsman that they wore solar topees instead of caps to protect themselves from the ball as much as the sun. Naoomal Jeoomal top edged a Clark bouncer into his head in the third Test, was unable to continue and didn't bat in the second innings.

Australia won the first Test of the 1934 Ashes series by 238 runs at Trent Bridge. Clarrie Grimmett took 25 wickets in the series, and Bill O‘Reilly 28 as England were spun to defeat. Bradman made 758 runs in the Tests and 2020 on the tour, with Stan McCabe making 2078. Patsy Hendren(132) and Maurice Leyland (153) ensured a draw at Old Trafford and England did manage a rare Test win over Australia at Lord's with Hedley Verity taking 14 wickets in a day and 15 in the match. Bradman (304) and Ponsford (181) put on 388 at Headingley and then 451 at the Oval where England lost by a massive 562 runs. Ponsford scored 266 in his last Test. Nobby Clark bowled some 'leg theory‘ against the Australians, with little success. Bill Voce took 8 for 66 for Notts against the Australians but withdrew from the attack with a 'leg injury‘ after Woodfall raised discrete objections.

England toured the West Indies in 1934/5 and showed the folly of sending a weakened team as they lost the rubber 2–1 with George Headley scoring 270 not out in the 4th Test at Sabina Park. South Africa won on English soil for the first time, taking the 5 Test series 1–0 in 1935 with a victory at Lord's by 157 runs thanks to Bruce Mitchell's 164 and Jock Cameron's quickfire 90. Cameron died at 30, of enteric fever, soon after returning home from this tour.

India used 22 players in three Tests in England in 1936. A then record 588 runs were scored on the second day of the Old Trafford Test and England too experimented with their team and took the rubber 2–0.

The 1936/37 Ashes tour, under Gubby Allen, was a titanic struggle. England, helped by rain freshening the pitch, won by 322 runs in Brisbane and an innings in Sydney where Wally Hammond scored 271 not out. Bill Voce was their spearhead, taking 17 wickets in these two games. Bradman added a record 346 for the sixth wicket with Jack Fingleton at Melbourne and followed that with 212 at Adelaide where his team leveled the score at 2–2. Bradman, McCabe and Badcock all scored hundreds in the decider at Melbourne and Australian took the series 3–2.

England beat New Zealand 1–0 in a three Test rubber in 1937. Tom Goddard took 6 for 29 in bowling out the visitors for 134 at the Old Trafford Test as they chased 265 to win. Jack Cowie had taken 6 for 67 for New Zealand and 10 in the match. Len Hutton scored a century after having begun his England career with 0 and 1 at Lords. Prospective tours of South Africa and West Indies fell through in the winter of 1937/38.

The 1938 Ashes series was a high scoring affair. Hutton, Barnett, Paynter (216*) and Compton made hundreds at Trent Bridge with the Australians scoring three including Stan McCabe's brilliant 232.

Hammond scored 240 in the Lord's Test while Bill Brown made a double ton and Bradman a match saving century for Australia. Old Trafford fell victim to the rain and Australia retained the Ashes with a win at Headingley, thanks to Bradman's century and 10 wickets for O'Reilly and 7 for Fleetwood-Smith. England won the final Test at the Oval thanks to a record Test score of 903 – 7 dec and Len Hutton's world record of 364 in 13 hours, 17 minutes. Bradman, whose score of 334 had been surpassed, was the first to congratulate the 22-year-old Yorkshireman. Maurice Leyland made 187 and the elegant Joe Hardstaff 169 not out. Australia subsided to 201 and 123, batting 2 short, and England won by an innings and 579.

Paul Gibb scored 93 and 106 on debut at Johannesburg on England's 1938/39 tour. England scored 11 centuries in the series and South Africa 6. Paynter scored 117 and 100 in the first Test and 243 in the third at Durban. England, 1–0, in the series, returned to Durban to play a deciding 'timeless' Test to the finish. It was abandoned as a draw after 10 days as England had to catch the train to catch the boat home. Needing 696 to win they were, incredibly, 654 for 5, Gibb having scored 120, Hammond 140 and Edrich 219. A record 1981 runs were scored, and the concept of timeless Tests was abandoned.

The three Tests between England and the West Indies in 1939 were the last before the Second World War, although a team for an MCC tour of India was selected more in hope than expectation of the matches being played. Len Hutton and Denis Compton, leaders of the bright new batting generation, scored hundreds at Lords where the brilliant George Headley scored a ton in each innings. Hammond became the first fielder to hold 100 Test catches at Old Trafford. England took the series 1–0 as the war clouds loomed over Europe.

CHAPTER FOUR

What Is Cricket ?

- What Is Cricket ?

Cricket is a bat-and-ball game played between two teams of eleven players on a field at the centre of which is a 22-yard (20-metre) pitch with a wicket at each end, each comprising two bails balanced on three stumps. The game proceeds when a player on the fielding team, called the bowler, "bowls" (propels) the ball from one end of the pitch towards the wicket at the other end. The batting side's players score runs by striking the bowled ball with a bat and running between the wickets, while the bowling side tries to prevent this by keeping the ball within the field and getting it to either wicket, and dismiss each batter (so they are "out"). Means of dismissal include being bowled, when the ball hits the stumps and dislodges the bails, and by the fielding side either catching a hit ball before it touches the ground, or hitting a wicket with the ball before a batter can cross the crease line in front of the wicket to complete a run. When ten batters have been dismissed, the innings ends and the teams swap roles. The game is adjudicated by two umpires, aided by a third umpire and match referee in international matches.

Forms of cricket range from Twenty20, with each team batting for a single innings of 20 overs and the game generally lasting three hours, to Test matches played over five days. Traditionally cricketers play in all-white kit, but in limited overs cricket they wear club or team colours. In addition to the basic kit, some players wear protective gear to prevent injury caused by the ball, which is a hard, solid spheroid made of compressed leather with a slightly raised sewn seam enclosing a cork core layered with tightly wound string.

The earliest reference to cricket is in South East England in the mid-16th century. It spread globally with the expansion of the British Empire, with the first international matches in the second half of the 19th century. The game's governing body is the International Cricket Council (ICC), which has over 100 members, twelve of which are full members who play Test matches. The game's rules, the Laws of Cricket, are maintained by Marylebone Cricket Club (MCC) in London. The sport is followed primarily in South Asia, Australasia, the United Kingdom, southern Africa and the West Indies.Women's cricket, which is organised and played separately, has also achieved international standard. The most successful side playing international cricket is Australia, which has won seven One Day International trophies, including five World Cups, more than any other country and has been the top-rated Test side more than any other country.

- History of cricket to 1725

A medieval "club ball" game involving an underhand bowl towards a batter. Ball catchers are shown positioning themselves to catch a ball. Detail from the Canticles of Holy Mary, 13th century.

Cricket is one of many games in the "club ball" sphere that basically involve hitting a ball with a hand-held implement; others include baseball (which shares many similarities with cricket, both belonging in the more specific bat-and-ball games category), golf, hockey, tennis, squash, badminton and table tennis. In cricket's case, a key difference is the existence of a solid target structure, the wicket (originally, it is thought, a "wicket gate" through which sheep were herded), that the batter must defend. The cricket historian Harry Altham identified three "groups" of "club ball" games: the "hockey group", in which the ball is driven to and fro between two targets (the goals); the "golf group", in which the ball is driven towards an undefended target (the hole); and the "cricket group", in which "the ball is aimed at a mark (the wicket) and driven away from it".

It is generally believed that cricket originated as a children's game in the south-eastern counties of England, sometime during the medieval period.Although there are claims for prior dates, the earliest definite reference to cricket being played comes from evidence given at a court case in Guildford in January 1597 (Old Style), equating to January 1598 in the modern calendar. The case concerned ownership of a certain plot of land and the court heard the testimony of a 59-year-old coroner, John Derrick, who gave witness that.

Being a scholler in the ffree schoole of Guldeford hee and diverse of his fellows did runne and play there at creckett and other plaies.

Given Derrick's age, it was about half a century earlier when he was at school and so it is certain that cricket was being played c. 1550 by boys in Surrey. The view that it was originally a children's game is reinforced by Randle Cotgrave's 1611 English-French dictionary in which he defined the noun "crosse" as "the crooked staff wherewith boys play at cricket" and the verb form "crosser" as "to play at cricket".

One possible source for the sport's name is the Old English word "cryce" (or "cricc") meaning a crutch or staff. In Samuel Johnson's Dictionary, he derived cricket from "cryce, Saxon, a stick". In Old French, the word "criquet" seems to have meant a kind of club or stick. Given the strong medieval trade connections between south-east England and the County of Flanders when the latter belonged to the Duchy of Burgundy, the name may have been derived from the Middle Dutch (in use in Flanders at the time) "krick"(-e), meaning a stick (crook). Another possible source is the Middle Dutch word "krickstoel", meaning a long low stool used for kneeling in church and which resembled the long low wicket with two stumps used in early cricket. According to Heiner Gillmeister, a European language expert of Bonn University, "cricket" derives from the Middle Dutch phrase for hockey, met de (krik ket)sen (i.e., "with the stick chase"). Gillmeister has suggested that not only the name but also the sport itself may be of Flemish origin.

- Growth of amateur and professional cricket in England

Evolution of the cricket bat. The original "hockey stick" (left) evolved into the straight bat from c. 1760 when pitched delivery bowling began.

Although the main object of the game has always been to score the most runs, the early form of cricket differed from the modern game in certain key technical aspects; the North American variant of cricket known as wicket retained many of these aspects. The ball was bowled underarm by the bowler and along the ground towards a batter armed with a bat that in shape resembled a hockey stick; the batter defended a low, two-stump wicket; and runs were called notches because the scorers recorded them by notching tally sticks.

In 1611, the year Cotgrave's dictionary was published, ecclesiastical court records at Sidlesham in Sussex state that two parishioners, Bartholomew Wyatt and Richard Latter, failed to attend church on Easter Sunday because they were playing cricket. They were fined 12d each and ordered to do penance.This is the earliest mention of adult participation in cricket and it was around the same time that the earliest known organised inter-parish or village match was played – at Chevening, Kent. In 1624, a player called Jasper Vinall died after he was accidentally struck on the head during a match between two parish teams in Sussex.

Cricket remained a low-key local pursuit for much of the 17th century. It is known, through numerous references found in the records of ecclesiastical court cases, to have been proscribed at times by the Puritans before and during the Commonwealth. The problem was nearly always the issue of Sunday play as the Puritans considered cricket to be "profane" if played on the Sabbath, especially if large crowds or gambling were involved.

According to the social historian Derek Birley, there was a "great upsurge of sport after the Restoration" in 1660. Gambling on sport became a problem significant enough for Parliament to pass the 1664 Gambling Act, limiting stakes to £100 which was, in any case, a colossal sum exceeding the annual income of 99% of the population. Along with prizefighting, horse racing and blood sports, cricket was perceived to be a gambling sport.Rich patrons made matches for high stakes, forming teams in which they engaged the first professional players.By the end of the century, cricket had developed into a major sport that was spreading throughout England and was already being taken abroad by English mariners and colonisers – the earliest reference to cricket overseas is dated 1676. A 1697 newspaper report survives of "a great cricket match" played in Sussex "for fifty guineas apiece" – this is the earliest known contest that is generally considered a First Class match.

- The patrons, and other players from the social class known as the "gentry", began to classify themselves as "amateurs" to establish a clear distinction from the professionals, who were invariably members of the working class, even to the point of having separate changing and dining facilities. The gentry, including such high-ranking nobles as the Dukes of Richmond, exerted their honour code of noblesse oblige to claim rights of leadership in any sporting contests they took part in, especially as it was necessary for them to play alongside their "social inferiors" if they were to win their bets. In time, a perception took hold that the typical amateur who played in first-class cricket, until 1962 when amateurism was abolished, was someone with a public school education who had then gone to one of Cambridge or Oxford University – society insisted that such people were "officers and gentlemen" whose destiny was to provide leadership. In a purely financial sense, the cricketing amateur would theoretically claim expenses for playing while his professional counterpart played under contract and was paid a wage or match fee; in practice, many amateurs claimed more than actual expenditure and the derisive term "shamateur" was coined to describe the practice.

- The Young Cricketer, 1768

The game underwent major development in the 18th century to become England's national sport.Its success was underwritten by the twin necessities of patronage and betting. Cricket was prominent in London as early as 1707 and, in the middle years of the century, large crowds flocked to matches on the Artillery Ground in Finsbury. The single wicket form of the sport attracted huge crowds and wagers to match, its popularity peaking in the 1748 season. Bowling underwent an evolution around 1760 when bowlers began to pitch the ball instead of rolling or skimming it towards the batter. This caused a revolution in bat design because, to deal with the bouncing ball, it was necessary to introduce the modern straight bat in place of the old "hockey stick" shape.

The Hambledon Club was founded in the 1760s and, for the next twenty years until the formation of Marylebone Cricket Club (MCC) and the opening of Lord's Old Ground in 1787, Hambledon was both the game's greatest club and its focal point. MCC quickly became the sport's premier club and the custodian of the Laws of Cricket. New Laws introduced in the latter part of the 18th century included the three stump wicket and leg before wicket (lbw).

The 19th century saw underarm bowling superseded by first roundarm and then overarm bowling. Both developments were controversial.Organisation of the game at county level led to the creation of the county clubs, starting with Sussex in 1839. In December 1889, the eight leading county clubs formed the official County Championship, which began in 1890.

The most famous player of the 19th century was W. G. Grace, who started his long and influential career in 1865. It was especially during the career of Grace that the distinction between amateurs and professionals became blurred by the existence of players like him who were nominally amateur but, in terms of their financial gain, de facto professional. Grace himself was said to have been paid more money for playing cricket than any professional.

The last two decades before the First World War have been called the "Golden Age of cricket". It is a nostalgic name prompted by the collective sense of loss resulting from the war, but the period did produce some great players and memorable matches, especially as organised competition at county and Test level developed.

- Cricket becomes an international sport

In 1844, the first-ever international match took place between the United States and Canada. In 1859, a team of English players went to North America on the first overseas tour. Meanwhile, the British Empire had been instrumental in spreading the game overseas and by the middle of the 19th century it had become well established in Australia, the Caribbean, India, Pakistan, New Zealand, North America and South Africa.

In 1862, an English team made the first tour of Australia. The first Australian team to travel overseas consisted of Aboriginal stockmen who toured England in 1868. The first One Day International match was played on 5 January 1971 between Australia and England at the Melbourne Cricket Ground.

In 1876–77, an England team took part in what was retrospectively recognised as the first-ever Test match at the Melbourne Cricket Ground against Australia. The rivalry between England and Australia gave birth to The Ashes in 1882, and this has remained Test cricket's most famous contest. Test cricket began to expand in 1888–89 when South Africa played England.

- World cricket in the 20th century

The inter-war years were dominated by Australia's Don Bradman, statistically the greatest Test batter of all time. Test cricket continued to expand during the 20th century with the addition of the West Indies (1928),

New Zealand (1930) and India (1932) before the Second World War and then Pakistan (1952), Sri Lanka (1982), Zimbabwe (1992), Bangladesh (2000), Ireland and Afghanistan (both 2018) in the post-war period. South Africa was banned from international cricket from 1970 to 1992 as part of the apartheid boycott.

- The rise of limited overs cricket

Cricket entered a new era in 1963 when English counties introduced the limited overs variant. As it was sure to produce a result, limited overs cricket was lucrative and the number of matches increased. The first Limited Overs International was played in 1971 and the governing International Cricket Council (ICC), seeing its potential, staged the first limited overs Cricket World Cup in 1975. In the 21st century, a new limited overs form, Twenty20, made an immediate impact. On 22 June 2017, Afghanistan and Ireland became the 11th and 12th ICC full members, enabling them to play Test cricket.

- A typical cricket field.

In cricket, the rules of the game are specified in a code called The Laws of Cricket (hereinafter called "the Laws") which has a global remit. There are 42 Laws (always written with a capital "L"). The earliest known version of the code was drafted in 1744 and, since 1788, it has been owned and maintained by its custodian, the Marylebone Cricket Club (MCC) in London.

- Playing area

Cricket is a bat-and-ball game played on a cricket field between two teams of eleven players each. The field is usually circular or oval in shape and the edge of the playing area is marked by a boundary, which may be a fence, part of the stands, a rope, a painted line or a combination of these; the boundary must if possible be marked along its entire length.

In the approximate centre of the field is a rectangular pitch (see image, below) on which a wooden target called a wicket is sited at each end; the wickets are placed 22 yards (20 m) apart. The pitch is a flat surface 10 feet (3.0 m) wide, with very short grass that tends to be worn away as the game progresses (cricket can also be played on artificial surfaces, notably matting). Each wicket is made of three wooden stumps topped by two bails.

- Cricket pitch and creases

As illustrated above, the pitch is marked at each end with four white painted lines: a bowling crease, a popping crease and two return creases. The three stumps are aligned centrally on the bowling crease, which is eight feet eight inches long. The popping crease is drawn four feet in front of the bowling crease and parallel to it; although it is drawn as a twelve-foot line (six feet either side of the wicket), it is, in fact, unlimited in length. The return creases are drawn at right angles to the popping crease so that they intersect the ends of the bowling crease; each return crease is drawn as an eight-foot line, so that it extends four feet behind the bowling crease, but is also, in fact, unlimited in length.

Before a match begins, the team captains (who are also players) toss a coin to decide which team will bat first and so take the first innings. Innings is the term used for each phase of play in the match.In each innings, one team bats, attempting to score runs, while the other team bowls and fields the ball, attempting to restrict the scoring and dismiss the batters. When the first innings ends, the teams change roles; there can be two to four innings depending upon the type of match. A match with four scheduled innings is played over three to five days; a match with two scheduled innings is usually completed in a single day. During an innings, all eleven members of the fielding team take the field, but usually only two members of the batting team are on the field at any given time. The exception to this is if a batter has any type of illness or injury restricting his or her ability to run, in this case the batter is allowed a runner who can run between the wickets when the batter hits a scoring run or runs,though this does not apply in international cricket. The order of batters is usually announced just before the match, but it can be varied.

The main objective of each team is to score more runs than their opponents but, in some forms of cricket, it is also necessary to dismiss all of the opposition batters in their final innings in order to win the match, which would otherwise be drawn. If the team batting last is all out having scored fewer runs than their opponents, they are said to have "lost by n runs" (where n is the difference between the aggregate number of runs scored by the teams). If the team that bats last scores enough runs to win, it is said to have "won by n wickets", where n is the number of wickets left to fall. For example, a team that passes its opponents‘ total having lost six wickets (i.e., six of their batters have been dismissed) have won the match "by four wickets".

In a two-innings-a-side match, one team's combined first and second innings total may be less than the other side's first innings total. The team with the greater score is then said to have "won by an innings and n runs", and does not need to bat again: n is the difference between the two teams' aggregate scores. If the team batting last is all out, and both sides have scored the same number of runs, then the match is a tie; this result is quite rare in matches of two innings a side with only 62 happening in first-class matches from the earliest known instance in 1741 until January 2017. In the traditional form of the game, if the time allotted for the match expires before either side can win, then the game is declared a draw.

If the match has only a single innings per side, then a maximum number of overs applies to each innings. Such a match is called a "limited overs" or "one-day" match, and the side scoring more runs wins regardless of the number of wickets lost, so that a draw cannot occur. In some cases, ties are broken by having each team bat for a one-over innings known as a Super Over; subsequent Super Overs may be played if the first Super Over ends in a tie. If this kind of match is temporarily interrupted by bad weather, then a complex mathematical formula, known as the Duckworth–Lewis–Stern method after its developers, is often used to recalculate a new target score. A one-day match can also be declared a "no-result" if fewer than a previously agreed number of overs have been bowled by either team, in circumstances that make normal resumption of play impossible; for example, wet weather.

In all forms of cricket, the umpires can abandon the match if bad light or rain makes it impossible to continue. There have been instances of entire matches, even Test matches scheduled to be played over five days, being lost to bad weather without a ball being bowled: for example, the third Test of the 1970/71 series in Australia.

- Innings

The innings (ending with 's' in both singular and plural form) is the term used for each phase of play during a match. Depending on the type of match being played, each team has either one or two innings. Sometimes all eleven members of the batting side take a turn to bat but, for various reasons, an innings can end before they have all done so. The innings terminates if the batting team is "all out", a term defined by the Laws: "at the fall of a wicket or the retirement of a batter, further balls remain to be bowled but no further batter is available to come in". In this situation, one of the batters has not been dismissed and is termed not out; this is because he has no partners left and there must always be two active batters while the innings is in progress.

- An innings may end early while there are still two not out batters

the batting team's captain may declare the innings closed even though some of his players have not had a turn to bat: this is a tactical decision by the captain, usually because he believes his team have scored sufficient runs and need time to dismiss the opposition in their innings

the set number of overs (i.e., in a limited overs match) have been bowled

the match has ended prematurely due to bad weather or running out of time

in the final innings of the match, the batting side has reached its target and won the game.

- Overs

The Laws state that, throughout an innings, "the ball shall be bowled from each end alternately in overs of 6 balls". The name "over" came about because the umpire calls "Over!" when six balls have been bowled. At this point, another bowler is deployed at the other end, and the fielding side changes ends while the batters do not. A bowler cannot bowl two successive overs, although a bowler can (and usually does) bowl alternate overs, from the same end, for several overs which are termed a "spell". The batters do not change ends at the end of the over, and so the one who was non-striker is now the striker and vice versa. The umpires also change positions so that the one who was at "square leg" now stands behind the wicket at the non-striker's end and vice versa.

- Clothing and equipment

English cricketer W. G. Grace "taking guard" in 1883. His pads and bat are very similar to those used today. The gloves have evolved somewhat. Many modern players use more defensive equipment than were available to Grace, most notably helmets and arm guards.

The wicket-keeper (a specialised fielder behind the batter) and the batters wear protective gear because of the hardness of the ball, which can be delivered at speeds of more than 145 kilometres per hour (90 mph) and presents a major health and safety concern. Protective clothing includes pads (designed to protect the knees and shins), batting gloves or wicket-keeper's gloves for the hands, a safety helmet for the head and a box for male players inside the trousers (to protect the crotch area). Some batters wear additional padding inside their shirts and trousers such as thigh pads, arm pads, rib protectors and shoulder pads. The only fielders allowed to wear protective gear are those in positions very close to the batter (i.e., if they are alongside or in front of him), but they cannot wear gloves or external leg guards.

Subject to certain variations, on-field clothing generally includes a collared shirt with short or long sleeves; long trousers; woolen pullover (if needed); cricket cap (for fielding) or a safety helmet; and spiked shoes or boots to increase traction. The kit is traditionally all white and this remains the case in Test and first-class cricket but, in limited overs cricket, team colours are worn instead.

- Bat and ball

Two types of cricket ball, both of the same size:

i) A used white ball. White balls are mainly used in limited overs cricket, especially in matches played at night, under floodlights (left).

ii) A used red ball. Red balls are used in Test cricket, first-class cricket and some other forms of cricket (right).

The essence of the sport is that a bowler delivers (i.e., bowls) the ball from his or her end of the pitch towards the batter who, armed with a bat, is "on strike" at the other end (see next sub-section: Basic gameplay).

The bat is made of wood, usually Salix alba (white willow), and has the shape of a blade topped by a cylindrical handle. The blade must not be more than 4.25 inches (10.8 cm) wide and the total length of the bat not more than 38 inches (97 cm). There is no standard for the weight, which is usually between 2 lb 7 oz and 3 lb (1.1 and 1.4 kg).

The ball is a hard leather-seamed spheroid, with a circumference of 9 inches (23 cm). The ball has a "seam": six rows of stitches attaching the leather shell of the ball to the string and cork interior. The seam on a new ball is prominent and helps the bowler propel it in a less predictable manner. During matches, the quality of the ball deteriorates to a point where it is no longer usable; during the course of this deterioration, its behaviour in flight will change and can influence the outcome of the match. Players will, therefore, attempt to modify the ball's behaviour by modifying its physical properties. Polishing the ball and wetting it with sweat or saliva is legal, even when the polishing is deliberately done on one side only to increase the ball's swing through the air, but the acts of rubbing other substances into the ball, scratching the surface or picking at the seam are illegal ball tampering.

- Player roles

Basic gameplay: bowler to batter

During normal play, thirteen players and two umpires are on the field. Two of the players are batters and the rest are all eleven members of the fielding team. The other nine players in the batting team are off the field in the pavilion. The image with overlay below shows what is happening when a ball is being bowled and which of the personnel are on or close to the pitch.

- Return crease

In the photo, the two batters (3 & 8; wearing yellow) have taken position at each end of the pitch (6). Three members of the fielding team (4, 10 & 11; wearing dark blue) are in shot. One of the two umpires (1; wearing white hat) is stationed behind the wicket (2) at the bowler's (4) end of the pitch. The bowler (4) is bowling the ball (5) from his end of the pitch to the batter at the other end who is called the "striker". The other batter (3) at the bowling end is called the "non-striker". The wicket-keeper (10), who is a specialist, is positioned behind the striker's wicket (9) and behind him stands one of the fielders in a position called "first slip" (11). While the bowler and the first slip are wearing conventional kit only, the two batters and the wicket-keeper are wearing protective gear including safety helmets, padded gloves and leg guards (pads).

While the umpire (1) in shot stands at the bowler's end of the pitch, his colleague stands in the outfield, usually in or near the fielding position called "square leg", so that he is in line with the popping crease (7) at the striker's end of the pitch. The bowling crease (not numbered) is the one on which the wicket is located between the return creases (12). The bowler (4) intends to hit the wicket (9) with the ball (5) or, at least, to prevent the striker (8) from scoring runs. The striker (8) intends, by using his bat, to defend his wicket and, if possible, to hit the ball away from the pitch in order to score runs.

Some players are skilled in both batting and bowling, or as either or these as well as wicket-keeping, so are termed all-rounders. Bowlers are classified according to their style, generally as fast bowlers, seam bowlers or spinners. Batters are classified according to whether they are right-handed or left-handed.

- Fielding

Of the eleven fielders, three are in shot in the image above. The other eight are elsewhere on the field, their positions determined on a tactical basis by the captain or the bowler. Fielders often change position between deliveries, again as directed by the captain or bowler.

If a fielder is injured or becomes ill during a match, a substitute is allowed to field instead of him, but the substitute cannot bowl or act as a captain, except in the case of concussion substitutes in international cricket. The substitute leaves the field when the injured player is fit to return. The Laws of Cricket were updated in 2017 to allow substitutes to act as wicket-keepers.

- Bowling and dismissal

Glenn McGrath of Australia holds the world record for most wickets in the Cricket World Cup.

Most bowlers are considered specialists in that they are selected for the team because of their skill as a bowler, although some are all-rounders and even specialist batters bowl occasionally. The specialists bowl several times during an innings but may not bowl two overs consecutively. If the captain wants a bowler to "change ends", another bowler must temporarily fill in so that the change is not immediate.

A bowler reaches his delivery stride by means of a "run-up" and an over is deemed to have begun when the bowler starts his run-up for the first delivery of that over, the ball then being "in play".

Fast bowlers, needing momentum, take a lengthy run up while bowlers with a slow delivery take no more than a couple of steps before bowling. The fastest bowlers can deliver the ball at a speed of over 145 kilometres per hour (90 mph) and they sometimes rely on sheer speed to try to defeat the batter, who is forced to react very quickly.

Other fast bowlers rely on a mixture of speed and guile by making the ball seam or swing (i.e. curve) in flight. This type of delivery can deceive a batter into miscuing his shot, for example, so that the ball just touches the edge of the bat and can then be "caught behind" by the wicket-keeper or a slip fielder. At the other end of the bowling scale is the spin bowler who bowls at a relatively slow pace and relies entirely on guile to deceive the batter. A spinner will often "buy his wicket" by "tossing one up" (in a slower, steeper parabolic path) to lure the batter into making a poor shot. The batter has to be very wary of such deliveries as they are often "flighted" or spun so that the ball will not behave quite as he expects and he could be "trapped" into getting himself out. In between the pacemen and the spinners are the medium paced seamers who rely on persistent accuracy to try to contain the rate of scoring and wear down the batter's concentration.

There are nine ways in which a batter can be dismissed: five relatively common and four extremely rare. The common forms of dismissal are bowled, caught, leg before wicket (lbw), run out and stumped. Rare methods are hit wicket,hit the ball twice, obstructing the field and timed out. The Laws state that the fielding team, usually the bowler in practice, must appeal for a dismissal before the umpire can give his decision. If the batter is out, the umpire raises a forefinger and says "Out!"; otherwise, he will shake his head and say "Not out".There is, effectively, a tenth method of dismissal, retired out, which is not an on-field dismissal as such but rather a retrospective one for which no fielder is credited.

- Batting, runs and extras

The directions in which a right-handed batter, facing down the page, intends to send the ball when playing various cricketing shots. The diagram for a left-handed batter is a mirror image of this one.

Batters take turns to bat via a batting order which is decided beforehand by the team captain and presented to the umpires, though the order remains flexible when the captain officially nominates the team. Substitute batters are generally not allowed, except in the case of concussion substitutes in international cricket.

In order to begin batting the batter first adopts a batting stance. Standardly, this involves adopting a slight crouch with the feet pointing across the front of the wicket, looking in the direction of the bowler, and holding the bat so it passes over the feet and so its tip can rest on the ground near to the toes of the back foot.

A skilled batter can use a wide array of "shots" or "strokes" in both defensive and attacking mode. The idea is to hit the ball to the best effect with the flat surface of the bat's blade. If the ball touches the side of the bat it is called an "edge". The batter does not have to play a shot and can allow the ball to go through to the wicketkeeper. Equally, he does not have to attempt a run when he hits the ball with his bat. Batters do not always seek to hit the ball as hard as possible, and a good player can score runs just by making a deft stroke with a turn of the wrists or by simply "blocking" the ball but directing it away from fielders so that he has time to take a run. A wide variety of shots are played, the batter's repertoire including strokes named according to the style of swing and the direction aimed: e.g., "cut", "drive", "hook", "pull".

The batter on strike (i.e. the "striker") must prevent the ball hitting the wicket, and try to score runs by hitting the ball with his bat so that he and his partner have time to run from one end of the pitch to the other before the fielding side can return the ball. To register a run, both runners must touch the ground behind the popping crease with either their bats or their bodies (the batters carry their bats as they run). Each completed run increments the score of both the team and the striker.

- Sachin Tendulkar is the only player to have scored one hundred international centuries

The decision to attempt a run is ideally made by the batter who has the better view of the ball's progress, and this is communicated by calling: usually "yes", "no" or "wait". More than one run can be scored from a single hit: hits worth one to three runs are common, but the size of the field is such that it is usually difficult to run four or more. To compensate for this, hits that reach the boundary of the field are automatically awarded four runs if the ball touches the ground en route to the boundary or six runs if the ball clears the boundary without touching the ground within the boundary. In these cases the batters do not need to run. Hits for five are unusual and generally rely on the help of "overthrows" by a fielder returning the ball. If an odd number of runs is scored by the striker, the two batters have changed ends, and the one who was non-striker is now the striker. Only the striker can score individual runs, but all runs are added to the team's total.

Additional runs can be gained by the batting team as extras (called "sundries" in Australia) due to errors made by the fielding side. This is achieved in four ways: no-ball, a penalty of one extra conceded by the bowler if he breaks the rules; wide, a penalty of one extra conceded by the bowler if he bowls so that the ball is out of the batter's reach bye, an extra awarded if the batter misses the ball and it goes past the wicket-keeper and gives the batters time to run in the conventional way leg bye, as for a bye except that the ball has hit the batter's body, though not his bat. If the bowler has conceded a no-ball or a wide, his team incurs an additional penalty because that ball (i.e., delivery) has to be bowled again and hence the batting side has the opportunity to score more runs from this extra ball.

- Specialist roles

Captain (cricket) and Wicket-keeper

The captain is often the most experienced player in the team, certainly the most tactically astute, and can possess any of the main skillsets as a batter, a bowler or a wicket-keeper. Within the Laws, the captain has certain responsibilities in terms of nominating his players to the umpires before the match and ensuring that his players conduct themselves "within the spirit and traditions of the game as well as within the Laws".

The wicket-keeper (sometimes called simply the "keeper") is a specialist fielder subject to various rules within the Laws about his equipment and demeanour. He is the only member of the fielding side who can effect a stumping and is the only one permitted to wear gloves and external leg guards. Depending on their primary skills, the other ten players in the team tend to be classified as specialist batters or specialist bowlers. Generally, a team will include five or six specialist batters and four or five specialist bowlers, plus the wicket-keeper.

- Umpires and scorers

The game on the field is regulated by the two umpires, one of whom stands behind the wicket at the bowler's end, the other in a position called "square leg" which is about 15–20 metres away from the batter on strike and in line with the popping crease on which he is taking guard. The umpires have several responsibilities including adjudication on whether a ball has been correctly bowled (i.e., not a no-ball or a wide); when a run is scored; whether a batter is out (the fielding side must first appeal to the umpire, usually with the phrase "How's that?" or "Owzat?"); when intervals start and end; and the suitability of the pitch, field and weather for playing the game. The umpires are authorised to interrupt or even abandon a match due to circumstances likely to endanger the players, such as a damp pitch or deterioration of the light.

Off the field in televised matches, there is usually a third umpire who can make decisions on certain incidents with the aid of video evidence. The third umpire is mandatory under the playing conditions for Test and Limited Overs International matches played between two ICC full member countries. These matches also have a match referee whose job is to ensure that play is within the Laws and the spirit of the game.

The match details, including runs and dismissals, are recorded by two official scorers, one representing each team. The scorers are directed by the hand signals of an umpire . For example, the umpire raises a forefinger to signal that the batter is out (has been dismissed); he raises both arms above his head if the batter has hit the ball for six runs. The scorers are required by the Laws to record all runs scored, wickets taken and overs bowled; in practice, they also note significant amounts of additional data relating to the game.

A match's statistics are summarised on a scorecard. Prior to the popularisation of scorecards, most scoring was done by men sitting on vantage points cuttings notches on tally sticks and runs were originally called notches.According to Rowland Bowen, the earliest known scorecard templates were introduced in 1776 by T. Pratt of Sevenoaks and soon came into general use.It is believed that scorecards were printed and sold at Lord's for the first time in 1846.

- thank you for buy & read this book

have a great day of your
from : Mr Vivek Kumar Pandey

- This All Credit Goes To My Super Hero Daddy. "Always Love You dad'.

Printed by Libri Plureos GmbH in Hamburg,
Germany